Cambridge Elements ≡

Elements in Generative Syntax
edited by
Robert Freidin
Princeton University

CONTROL

Idan Landau
Tel Aviv University

CAMBRIDGE
UNIVERSITY PRESS

Shaftesbury Road, Cambridge CB2 8EA, United Kingdom

One Liberty Plaza, 20th Floor, New York, NY 10006, USA

477 Williamstown Road, Port Melbourne, VIC 3207, Australia

314–321, 3rd Floor, Plot 3, Splendor Forum, Jasola District Centre,
New Delhi – 110025, India

103 Penang Road, #05–06/07, Visioncrest Commercial, Singapore 238467

Cambridge University Press is part of Cambridge University Press & Assessment,
a department of the University of Cambridge.

We share the University's mission to contribute to society through the pursuit of
education, learning and research at the highest international levels of excellence.

www.cambridge.org
Information on this title: www.cambridge.org/9781009532815

DOI: 10.1017/9781009243124

First published 2024

A catalogue record for this publication is available from the British Library

ISBN 978-1-009-53281-5 Hardback
ISBN 978-1-009-24311-7 Paperback
ISSN 2635-0726 (online)
ISSN 2635-0718 (print)

Control

Elements in Generative Syntax

DOI: 10.1017/9781009243124
First published online: November 2024

Idan Landau
Tel Aviv University

Author for correspondence: Idan Landau, idanlan@tauex.tau.ac.il

Abstract: This Element presents the major findings and theoretical advances in the area of control. The different types of control (complement, adjunct, obligatory, nonobligatory) are described and their profiles in several languages are illustrated. It is shown that while certain features of obligatory control (OC) are common – nullness of PRO, nonfinite complements – they are not universal, and hence should not enter its core definition. Comparing approaches to the choice of controller based on lexical meaning postulates with those based on embedding of speech acts, it is concluded that the latter provide deeper insights into the core properties of OC. The fundamental semantic distinction between clauses denoting a property and those denoting a proposition proves to be important: It affects both the possibility of partial control in complements and the possibility of nonobligatory control in adjuncts. These insights are integrated in the Two-Tiered Theory of Control, laid out in the final sections.

Keywords: generative syntax, control, predication, infinitives, adjuncts

ISBNs: 9781009532815 (HB), 9781009243117 (PB), 9781009243124 (OC)
ISSNs: 2635-0726 (online), 2635-0718 (print)

Contents

1 Introduction

The syntax and interpretation of subordinate nonfinite clauses have been a topic of analysis from the earliest works of generative grammar. Sentences involving what we call today control (the term is due to Postal 1970) have figured in the earliest works of generative grammar (see Chomsky 1955: 246–250, 1965: 22–24). The reason was that they illustrate a curious mismatch between form and meaning, a fundamental concern of the discipline from the outset: A single noun phrase (NP) in the matrix clause appears to be semantically associated both with the matrix predicate and with the embedded predicate.

To illustrate, the single NP *Tom* in (1a) is associated with the semantic role of "wanter" (subject of the main clause) and the agent of *finish* (subject of subordinate clause). Likewise in (1b), *Tom* is associated with the semantic role of the addressee of *tell* and the agent of *finish*.

(1)　a.　Tom wanted to finish the job.
　　　b.　Helen told Tom to finish the job.

There is clear evidence that the NP *Tom* occurs in the main clause in (1a) and (1b). Thus, its semantic relation to the main verbs *want* and *tell* is unproblematic. But how can it be related to the embedded verb *finish*? A key idea has been that this relation is indirect. It is not *Tom* that is related to *finish*, but an "invisible" (null) NP, serving as the subject of the subordinate clause. To be maximally neutral about the nature of this null subject, we can notate it as Δ. It is customary to label these constructions according to the grammatical function of the matrix argument chosen as the antecedent of the embedded subject: *subject control* in (2a) and *object control* in (2b).

(2)　a.　Tom$_i$ wanted [Δ_i to finish the job].　　*Subject control*
　　　b.　Helen told Tom$_i$ [Δ_i to finish the job].　*Object control*

How is Δ related to *Tom*? Intuitively, Δ refers to *Tom*; this coreference is represented as coindexing. But how is this relation established in the grammar? This is the fundamental question of control, the relation holding between the controller (*Tom*) and the controllee (Δ).

Throughout the years, this analysis has split into a number of more specific research questions, each generating a large body of scholarship.[1]

---

[1] Control has been extensively studied within Categorial Grammar, Lexical Functional Grammar, Head-Driven Phrase-Structure Grammar, Government and Binding, Minimalism, Formal Semantics, and Cognitive Grammar. A single Element cannot hope to cover the vastness of this literature, so my present goal is rather modest: discuss the major approaches to control, grouped into a few super-categories, and show how they inform and lead to our current understanding of control phenomena. For previous surveys on the topic of control, covering much of its history, see Davies and Dubinsky (2004), Stiebels (2007, 2015), Kirby et al. (2010), Landau (2013), Polinsky

(3)   Fundamental questions of control theory
   a. What is the nature of the controlled category?
      Is it a semantic variable, a θ-role, a null pronoun/reflexive, or a copy?
      In Section 3.1, I will discuss evidence for a syntactic answer – the controllee is
      a kind of a null pronoun (often labeled "PRO").
   b. What is the nature of the relation between the controller and the controllee?
      Is it syntactic, lexical-semantic, pragmatic, or a combination thereof?
      Section 3 surveys three families of theories that approach the answer from
      these three angles.
   c. How is the controller determined?
      By lexical entailments, by syntactic locality, by principles of speech acts, or
      by logophoric prominence? Partial answers to this hard question will be
      offered in Sections 3.2 and 3.3.

By assumption, PRO functions as a standard subject in the complement clause. Indeed, PRO is fully active syntactically, as documented in Landau (2013: chapter 3): It binds anaphors, saturates secondary predicates, triggers agreement, and bears case (on case-marked PRO, see Landau 2006, 2008, Bobaljik and Landau 2009), in ways that implicit, nonsyntactic arguments cannot. These findings already limit potential answers to question (3a) insofar as they rule out a purely lexical/semantic conception of the controllee. However, they leave open the possibility of an *overt* controllee, alternating with PRO or even taking its place (see Section 3.1).

The theory to be articulated in this Element is the Two-Tiered Theory of Control (TTC; Landau 2015, 2018, 2020, 2021a,b). This theory, presented in Section 5, builds on insights gathered from many previous studies, which are grouped into three main families in Section 3. The discussion of these precursors will serve to map out the empirical terrain in which the TTC should be grounded as well as the theoretical demands it should respond to. At its barest, the TTC claims that control is obtained in two different ways: predication and logophoric antecedence. In both, PRO is a λ-abstractor, turning the complement into a predicate. In predicative control, this predicate is directly applied to the controller Determiner Phrase (DP). In logophoric control, it applies to a null nominal at the left periphery of the complement, which is related to the controller DP by the doxastic counterpart relation ("*de se* counterpart"; Chierchia 1990, Anand 2006, Pearson 2013, 2016). These two routes of control are instantiated in complements of different predicates as well as in adjuncts; each gives rise to a distinct empirical profile, accounting for many puzzling (and seemingly contradictory) properties documented in previous literature. Furthermore, the notion of logophoric antecedence extends to Non-Obligatory Control (NOC) as well, as discussed in Section 4.

(2013), and Potsdam and Haddad (2017). The most extensive work to date is Landau (2013), whose footsteps I follow later.

The structure of this Element is as follows. Section 2 characterizes the key concept of Obligatory Control (OC) by highlighting its differences from both standard pronominal anaphora and from Raising. Section 3 discusses three families of theories of control: syntactic theories, lexical-semantic theories, and embedded speech act (ESA) theories. The classification is mainly heuristic, indicating which component of grammar is deemed the most relevant for establishing the control dependency. Section 4 discusses NOC, a category that turns out to be richer and more varied than traditionally assumed. Section 5 lays out the TTC, synthesized from Landau's recent works, and spells out its application to complements and adjuncts. Section 6 concludes with a list of lingering challenges for future research.

2 The Essence of Obligatory Control

OC is a referential dependency, but referential dependencies come in many different cloaks. A useful method of pinning down the essence of OC is to highlight the unique properties that set it apart from other referential dependencies. In Section 2.1, I discuss the OC signature, which distinguishes OC from standard pronominal anaphora. In Section 2.2, I discuss the main differences between OC and Raising. Together, these two sections characterize the notion of OC as understood and used in current research.

2.1 The OC Signature

Before any meaningful investigation of a grammatical construction can be carried out, one must delineate the class of phenomena that fall under this construction. Such "working definitions" are heuristic in nature. As knowledge accumulates, and as more languages enter the data pool, the working definitions change to reflect our better understanding of what is essential to the grammatical construction of interest and what is merely coincidental to it. In linguistic research, in fact, it is expected that later incarnations of the definitions will be sparser and more abstract than earlier ones. Typically, notions like linear order, overtness, and so on, initially taken to be essential, are subsequently discarded in view of cross-linguistic variability, and commonalities are gradually discerned at deeper levels.[2]

This has also been the fate of the notion of OC, first introduced in Williams (1980), which has undergone considerable revisions ever since.[3] As a starting point for current research, I will adopt *the OC signature* of Landau (2013), slightly adjusted to reflect some recent findings in the field.

---

[2] For a recent survey of the rich cross-linguistic terrain of OC, see Landau (2024).
[3] See Landau (2013: 34–38) for past criteria for OC that were found to be spurious.

(4)   *The OC signature*
      In a construction $[\ldots X_i \ldots [_S Y_i \ldots] \ldots]$, where Y is the subject of
      clause S, if:
      a.   X must be (a) codependent(s) of S, AND
      b.   Y (or part of it) must be interpreted as a bound variable
      then this is an *OC* construction (X = controller, Y = controllee).

In (4), the controller and controllee are neutrally labeled X and Y, rather than
DP and PRO, respectively. This is meant to allow implicit controllers, which do
not surface as overt DPs, and also to allow controllees that surface as overt
pronouns rather than as a null category (see Section 3.1). A "dependent" of S is
either an argument or an adjunct of S; thus, (4a) subsumes both complement
OC, where the controller and S are co-arguments, and adjunct OC (on the latter,
see Section 5.2). Condition (4a) does not require the controller to be unique, thus
allowing both control shift and split control, as long as the two potential controllers
are codependents (in effect, co-arguments) of S. Finally, the parentheses in (4b) are
meant to allow partial control (PC; see Section 3.1).

To illustrate with familiar examples, consider the following contrast.

(5)   a.   Venessa$_i$ was impressed that Mike$_j$ had tried [PRO$_{j/*i}$ to regain   *OC*
           his/*her composure].
      b.   Venessa$_i$ was impressed that Mike$_j$ had understood that   *NOC*
           [PRO$_{i/j}$ regaining his/her composure] was essential to the discussion.

Suppose that the examples in (5) are not drawn from English but from some
understudied language, and your goal as a linguist is to identify their nature with
respect to control. Based on informant judgments, you observe that in (5a),
Venessa and the bracketed clause are not codependents, and control fails;
whereas in (5b), both *Venessa* and *Mike* are not codependents of the bracketed
clause, and control goes through with either of them. This indicates that (5a)
abides by criterion (4a) and hence stands a good chance of instantiating OC,
while (5b) violates this criterion and so must be NOC. To strengthen this
conclusion, you can apply criterion (4b).

(6)   a. Only Mike tried to regain his composure.
      b. Only Mike understood that regaining his composure was essential
          to the discussion.

Imagine that Venessa and Bob also tried to bring it about that Mike regain his
composure. In this situation, (6a) is still true, because PRO must be understood
as a bound variable, and Mike is the only individual of whom the property
$\lambda x.\textbf{try}(x,\textbf{regain-composure}(x))$ holds. Hence, the complement of *try* passes
the second criterion of OC (4b) too. Imagine next that Venessa and Bob also
understood that Mike's regaining his composure was essential to the discussion.

On this scenario, (6b) has a false reading; namely, the reading that ascribes to Mike the property λx. **understood(x,essential-to-discussion(regaining-composure(Mike))).** The sentence is false because the PRO subject of the gerund *regaining his composure* is understood referentially (as *Mike*) and not as a bound variable; not only did Mike reach the relevant understanding concerning Mike, but so did Venessa and Bob. This indicates that the subject gerund in (6b) falls under NOC also with respect to criterion (4b).

The criteria in (4) are particularly useful in distinguishing OC from pronominal anaphora. Pronouns, including null pronouns, often take intrasentential antecedents, but the relation between the antecedent and the pronoun is looser than the one required by the OC signature. Nevertheless, there is one construction that is famously similar to OC, and which the criteria in (4) are too coarse to distinguish from OC: That is Raising. We now turn to the OC-Raising distinction.

2.2 OC versus Raising

In Raising constructions, a nominal that is thematically an argument of the embedded predicate appears in the matrix clause, due to A-movement. The Raising predicate itself assigns no θ-role to the raised nominal; that is why nonthematic arguments (expletives and idiom chunks) can appear in Raising but not in control constructions. An expletive cannot get any θ-role, being nonreferential. An idiom chunk must be interpreted within the idiomatic phrase. If separated from the idiomatic phrase by movement (= Raising), the idiom chunk is still interpretable in its base copy. In control, however, there is no copy of the controller inside the complement clause; hence, the idiom chunk is forced to be interpreted as an argument of the control predicate, leading to the loss of the idiomatic reading and often to anomalous interpretations.

Examples (7a) and (7b) show the compatibility of Raising-to-Subject predicates with expletives and idiom chunks, while (7c) and (7d) show the incompatibility of subject control predicates with these elements. Similarly (8a,b) versus (8c,d) show the parallel contrast between Raising-to-Object and object control predicates (see (2a) and (2b) for the distinction between subject and object control).[4]

(7) a. It seems that John is happy.
     b. My leg appeared to have been pulled.
     c. * It hoped that John is happy.
     d. * My leg attempted to be pulled.

---

[4] With verbs like *prevent*, *stop*, and *keep*, Raising-to-Object has an overt effect on word order, shifting the embedded subject to the left of *from*, which is likely a negative complementizer (Postal 1974, Postal and Pullum 1988, Landau 2002, Baltin 2009).

(8)   a.   We expect it to be snowing all weekend.
      b.   The police prevented tabs from being kept on their informer.
      c.   * We convinced it to be snowing all weekend.
      d.   * The police dissuaded tabs from being kept on their informer.

As noted, these differences reflect different syntactic derivations, corresponding to movement in the case of Raising as opposed to referential antecedence in the case of control. The raised nominal starts out in the embedded Spec, TP and raises to the matrix Spec,TP (in Raising-to-Subject) or the matrix Spec, VP (in Raising-to-Object); see (9a) and (9b). The controlled nominal, namely PRO, occupies the embedded Spec,TP position; see (9c) and (9d).

(9)   a.   Bill$_i$ appeared [$_{TP}$ ~~Bill~~$_i$ to feel better].   *Raising*
      b.   They expected$_k$ [$_{VP}$ Bill$_i$ t$_k$ [$_{TP}$ ~~Bill~~$_i$ to remain silent]].   *Raising*
      c.   Bill$_i$ hoped [$_{CP}$ [$_{TP}$ PRO$_i$ to feel better]].   *Control*
      d.   They convinced Bill [$_{CP}$ [$_{TP}$ PRO$_i$ to remain silent]].   *Control*

Accordingly, Raising and OC display a wide array of empirical contrasts beyond the familiar ones in (7) and (8).[5] These contrasts can be grouped into three categories. (i) Low thematic source: The raised nominal receives its θ-role in the lower clause, whereas the controller nominal receives its θ-role in the matrix clause. (ii) "Reconstruction": A raised nominal can take scope, or be bound, in its embedded copy position, whereas a controller nominal is necessarily interpreted in the matrix clause. (iii) Derivational history: The raised nominal displays properties of a copy in a movement chain, whereas the controller nominal does not.

Starting with (i), this is the source of the contrast in the tolerance to nonthematic arguments in (7) and (8). It is also the reason why lexical ("quirky") case assigned in the lower clause is preserved on a raised nominal but not on a controller. Quirky case can be seen as a morphological reflection of θ-assignment, hence its preservation in Raising indicates the low thematic source of the raised nominal. A minimal pair in Icelandic, taken from Sigurðsson (2008), is shown in (10) (see also Thráinsson 1979, Bobaljik and Landau 2009). The embedded passive verb "helped" assigns quirky DAT to its subject. This case lodges on PRO in the control complement (10a) and is *not* passed on to the controller DP (which is NOM). In contrast, the quirky DAT case moves along with the raised nominal in Raising (10b).

(10) a.   Mennirnir/*Mönnunum vonast   til [að PRO verða hjálpað].   *Control*
           men.the.NOM/*DAT   hope   for to   be   helped
           "The men hope to be both helped."

---
[5] For extensive comparisons, see Davies and Dubinsky (2004), Kirby et al. (2010), Landau (2013: 8–18), and Polinsky (2013).

b. Mönnunum/*Mennirnir   virðist [~~mönnunum~~ hafa verið hjálpað].   *Raising*
men.the.DAT/*NOM   seem   have been helped
"The men seem to have both been helped."

Consider (ii), "reconstruction" contrasts.[6] The raised nominal can be interpreted in its original merge position, but a controller must be interpreted in the matrix clause because it has no embedded copy (PRO is *not* a copy). This contrast shows up in many ways; we illustrate it here with scope reconstruction (11) and with Weak Crossover effects (12).[7]

(11) a.   Seven contestants are likely to lose on the next round.   *Raising*
           7con.≫ *likely, likely*≫*7con.*
      b.   Seven contestants are afraid to lose on the next round.   *Control*
           7con.≫ *afraid,* **afraid*> *7con.*

(12) a.   His$_i$ medical condition worries every patient$_i$.
      b.   His$_i$ medical condition seems to worry every patient$_i$.   *Raising*
      c.   * His$_i$ doctor tried to worry every patient$_i$.   *Control*

Such contrasts in reconstruction are consistently found in other languages as well (see Anagnostopoulou and Alexiadou 1999 on Greek, Wurmbrand 1999 on German, and Baykov and Rudnev 2020 on Russian).

Scope reconstruction in Raising allows the raised nominal to be interpreted *de dicto*, but a controller must be read *de re*. Under the *de dicto* reading, an indefinite nominal introduces an entity in the context of thought, hence there is no commitment to its existence in the actual world. Under the *de re* reading, an indefinite nominal introduces an entity in the context of utterance, hence it is assumed to exist in the actual world. This is reflected in the following contrast.

---

[6] I use the term descriptively to mean interpretation of a lower copy than the one pronounced, with no implication of a grammatical operation of "reconstruction."

[7] Truswell (2013) challenges the claim that controller QPs do not reconstruct, on the basis of interactions with embedded QPs. According to the judgments he provides in (i), inverse scope is marginally possible but only when the matrix QP is the controller (i-a,d). Indiscriminate QR out of control infinitives cannot account for this pattern; instead, Truswell proposes that the controller QP may take scope in the position of PRO.

(i)   a. Mary persuaded someone to read every book on the reading list.   ∃≫∀,%∀≫∃
      b. Someone persuaded Mary to read every book on the reading list.   ∃≫∀,*∀≫∃
      c. Mary promised someone to read every book on the reading list.   ∃≫∀,*∀≫∃
      d. Someone promised Mary to read every book on the reading list.   ∃≫∀,%∀≫∃

Truswell does not propose to conflate raising and control; rather, he argues that scope reconstruction should be extended to nonmovement dependencies as well. However, the facts in (11)/(13) and further scope interactions surveyed in the literature mentioned in the previous footnote pose considerable difficulties to this conclusion.

(13) a.   Smith expected a unicorn to drink the apple juice.   *Raising*
      b.   # Smith tempted a unicorn to drink the apple juice.   *Control*

Parallel contrasts in reconstruction emerge when the matrix QP interacts with a negative complementizer (Baltin 2009).

Finally, we turn to (iii), derivational history. Certain grammatical conditions are sensitive to whether a given syntactic position is derived (by movement) or not. For example, Rizzi's (1986) Chain Condition blocks A-movement across a coindexed reflexive clitic (a corollary of the Minimal Link Condition; Chomsky 1995), as in *$[DP_i \ldots si_i \ldots t_i]$. This correctly predicts that subject control across a (dative) reflexive clitic will be possible (14b) but Raising to subject will not (14a) (copies are marked as traces for expository purposes only). Note that (14b) is active and not passive, the "be" auxiliary occurring due to reflexivization.

(14) a. *I   due candidati$_i$ si_i risultavano [t$_i$ poter   vincere].
          the two candidates to.each-other   appeared   to.be.able   to.win
          ("The two candidates appeared to each other to be able to win.")
      b.   I   due concorrenti$_i$ si_i sono promessi [di PRO$_i$ essere leali].
          the two competitors to.each-other were promised DI   to.be loyal
          "The two competitors promised to each other to be loyal."

Another derivational constraint involves *Freezing* – the ban on extraction from derived positions (Wexler and Culicover 1980). It is an old observation that the postverbal nominal in *expect*-type constructions blocks subextraction (15a,b) but that in *persuade*-type construction does not (15c,d) (Chomsky 1973, Postal 1974, Runner 2006).

(15) a.   * Who$_i$ did you expect$_k$ [$_{VP}$ [stories about t$_i$]$_j$ t$_k$ [t$_j$ to terrify John]]?
            (cf. Who$_i$ did you hear [stories about t$_i$])?
      b.   * Who$_i$ did you find$_k$ [$_{VP}$ [pictures of t$_i$]$_j$ t$_k$ [t$_j$ to be offensive]]?
            (cf. Who$_i$ did you find [pictures of t$_i$]?)
      c.   Who$_i$ did you persuade$_k$ [$_{VP}$ [friends of t$_i$]$_j$ t$_k$ [PRO$_j$ to join us]]?
      d.   Who$_i$ did you push$_k$ [$_{VP}$ [friends of t$_i$]$_j$ t$_k$ [PRO$_j$ to reconsider their position]]?

While Chomsky (1973), assuming no Raising to Object, traced these facts to Subjacency (more currently, the Subject Condition), on the Raising analysis they follow from the Freezing Principle.

It is worth mentioning some Raising-Control contrasts that were thought to be solid but research has proven to be unreliable. One property that was traditionally associated with Raising is clause-"defectiveness." Within the GB theory of the 1980s, this idea was cashed out in terms of clause size: Raising clauses were analyzed as bare TPs, in contrast to control clauses, analyzed as ordinary CPs. However, this idea is dubious in both directions. First, restructuring gives rise to control complements smaller than CP in many languages (Wurmbrand 2015). Conversely, "hyper-raising" out of finite CPs is also attested in several languages (Wurmbrand 2019). While clause size often correlates with the Raising-Control contrast language-*internally*, it is not a criterion of universal validity.

A second property concerns potential overtness of the dependent position – the controllee or the Raising "trace." It is already known that overt Raising is unnecessary in null subject languages; the matrix subject position may remain null (or contain a null expletive), and the nominal remains unraised in its embedded base position (see Halpert 2019 for some theoretical implications). We also know that controllees may surface as overt pronouns (see Section 3.1). Finally, the phenomenon of backward control suggests that they can also surface as full lexical DPs (Polinsky and Potsdam 2002, Fukuda 2008, Potsdam 2009). Thus, how the control or Raising dependency is spelled out is not a reliable distinction between the two constructions. In contrast, the properties demonstrated in (8)–(15) provide a solid battery of contrasts that have been repeatedly confirmed in the literature throughout the years.

3 A General Road Map of OC Theories

Control is one of the earliest concerns of generative grammar, going back to Rosenbaum (1967). Six decades of research have produced a vast amount of findings as well as theoretical analyses. It is impossible to do justice to control theories in one Element. Instead, my strategy in this section will be to group the different proposals in three broad classes: syntactic theories, lexical-semantic theories, and (embedded) speech act theories. These categories are natural insofar as they trace the commonalities among disparate theories in the grammatical *module* these theories take as the essential locus of the control dependency (syntax, lexicon, or syntax-pragmatics interface), abstracting away from internal differences in which features the dependency hinges on. The categories are not mutually exclusive. It goes without saying that syntactic theories acknowledge the role of lexical information in determining configurational properties. Similarly, lexical theories do not necessarily deny the existence of PRO or its relevance to control. Rather, the classification is based on what the different theories take to be the *essential* component in explaining control.

This section has two further goals. First, to highlight the important insights gained over the years from the syntactic and lexicalist approaches. Second, to highlight their intrinsic limitations. Armed with this understanding, we will turn to the speech act approach, which represents the most recent and promising avenue of research into OC, to see how it handles the challenges left open by the previous approaches.

3.1 Syntactic Theories

The earliest account of OC in generative grammar was a syntactic one – The Equi-NP Deletion rule of Rosenbaum (1967, 1970). Both the relata of the rule – two identical NPs – and the rule itself were strictly syntax-internal. Moreover, the rule was subject to a syntactic locality principle – the Minimal Distance Principle (MDP) – which required the controller to be the closest NP to the controlled (deleted) NP. The MDP was revived in a PRO-based analysis by Larson (1991) (see also Martin 1996, Manzini and Roussou 2000). Within the Movement Theory of Control, the MDP was adopted as descriptively correct, its effects reduced to the Minimal Link Condition, specifically, the ban on A-movement across an intervening A-position (Hornstein 1999 and subsequent work).

The main ingredients of Rosenbaum's proposal have been rejected by subsequent research. This early work in the 1970s revealed that the controlled position manifests interpretive properties typical of pronouns rather than of lexical NPs (e.g., bound variable readings, split control); more fundamentally, the deletion analysis did not explain the fundamental effect of *obligatory* control, for it said nothing about why deletion is sometimes impossible (*John believed *(Mary) to be smart*), sometimes possible (*John wanted (Mary) to win*), and sometimes mandatory (*John managed (*Mary) to win*). Likewise, the MDP faced serious counterexamples from the outset, much beyond the familiar *promise*-example, which furthermore bore the unmistakable signature of *lexical* sensitivity, much to the detriment of a purely syntactic constraint. These matters have been discussed extensively elsewhere, so I do not elaborate on them here.[8] Interestingly, the classical Equi-NP analysis is reincarnated in Chomsky's recent "Form Copy" theory of control (Chomsky 2021, Chomsky et al. 2023, Chomsky 2024), which is predicated on the idea that lexical NPs can be rendered copies not just by movement, leading to deletion of the lower copy (see Landau to appear for a detailed critique of that proposal).

Nonetheless, the lingering heritage of the Equi-NP Deletion account was its most fundamental and yet nontrivial aspect: Superficially subjectless clauses do contain a subject at some abstract grammatical level. The nature of the abstractness was much debated in the following years, but current consensus retains the original idea that (barring reduced/restructuring complements) OC is indeed a dependence between two *syntactic* relata. The syntactic reality of PRO is

---

[8] For a historical and critical discussion of Equi-NP Deletion, see Landau (2013: 3–8). For extensive discussions of the problems with MDP-based analyses, see Landau (2013: 149–154), Culicover and Jackendoff (2001), and Jackendoff and Culicover (2003). Note that the decisive effect of mood particles on the choice of controllers in Japanese and Korean (Section 3.3) further demonstrates the inadequacy of the MDP.

revealed in a variety of interactions with syntactic processes, such as binding, agreement, and case concord (see Landau 2013: chapter 3).

Perhaps the most straightforward evidence for the syntactic reality of the controlled position is the fact that in many situations, across many languages, it *is* realized by an explicit nominal. One class of cases involves controlled overt pronouns. In several Niger-Congo languages, irrealis complements of volitional and implicative verbs display OC with an obligatory pronominal subject, as in the Gã example (16a) (Allotey 2021). In other languages, typically (but not only) in Romance, PRO alternates with an overt pronoun, but the alternation is semantically significant: The controlled overt pronoun is associated with exhaustive or contrastive focus, often accompanied by some focus-sensitive particle. Example (16b) is from Hungarian (Szabolcsi 2009).

(16) a. Gbekebii$_i$ lɛ   nye   [(ni) *(amei$_{i/*j}$) he   shia].
          Children   DET   manged COMP   3.PL   buy.INF home
          "The children managed to buy a home."

      b. Nem   felejtettem   el   [én   is   aláírni   a   levelet].
          Not   forgot.1SG   PFX   I   too   to.sign   the letter.ACC
          "I didn't forget to bring it about that I too sign the letter."

Controlled pronouns in Chirag Dargwa also require a focus particle, but in this language, the embedded subject may even surface as a conjunction, with the controlled pronoun (or long-distance reflexive) occurring as one conjunct, a rare case of *overt PC* (Ganenkov 2023); on PC, see Section 3.3.

Furthermore, in some languages, the controlled position can surface as a full DP, a phenomenon labeled *backward control* (Polinsky and Potsdam 2002, Fukuda 2008, Potsdam 2009): The embedded subject position hosts a lexical DP and the matrix controller position is null, yet reveals its syntactic reality by a number of tests. The pair in (17) illustrates an alternation between standard (forward) and backward control in Malagasy (LNK = linker, CT = circumstantial topic [voice], TT = theme topic [voice]), taken from Potsdam 2009: 765). Abstracting away from the extracted embedded object, in (17a) the controller occurs as the matrix object and surfaces with accusative case; in (17b), the controller occurs as the embedded subject and surfaces with nominative case.

(17) a. *Forward control*
          trano-n'   iza   no   naneren' i Mery ahy   [hofafana]?
          house-LNK   who   FOC force.CT Mary   1SG. ACC sweep.TT

      b. *Backward control*
          trano-n'   iza   no   naneren' i Mery [hofafa- ko]?
          house-LNK   who   FOC force.CT Mary   sweep.TT 1SG.NOM
          "Whose house did Mary force me to sweep?"

Pronominal control and backward control make two points eminently clear. First, OC cannot be fully reduced to a relation between a matrix predicate/ argument and a subjectless clause; there must be a way to establish OC with a *syntactic controllee*. Second, PRO and pronouns do not exhaust the spellout possibilities for controlled DPs. Backward control is most readily explained by the Movement Theory of Control (MTC) as an instance of "low spellout" in an A-chain, and it is still the strongest argument in its favor.[9] It should be noted, though, that backward control is quite tricky to demonstrate; several early proposals invoking it have been retracted or reanalyzed without it (Kwon et al. 2010, Yoshimoto 2013, Alexiadou and Anagnostopoulou 2021, Pietraszko 2021). The general validity of the MTC as a viable theory of control has been subject to much criticism from different angles. If backward control will ultimately be reanalyzed in one of the ways alluded to above or otherwise, the MTC will lose its main empirical motivation.[10]

Within minimalism, the other main syntactic approach to OC is the Agree-based account.[11] On this approach, PRO enters an Agree relation with a matrix element (directly or indirectly via the embedded Agr) and consequently values its ϕ-features; on some versions, it also values an indexical feature. This agreement chain is translated at LF as variable binding. Initially, this approach was designed to capture noncanonical phenomena like finite and partial control (on PC, see Section 3.1); however, subsequent work has shown that these phenomena can also be captured under alternative conceptions (e.g., Pearson 2016, Vinka 2022).

Finite control has been documented in a range of languages (all the Balkan languages, Persian, Kannada, Korean, Japanese, Arabic, Amharic, South Saami), challenging the classical view that linked control to nonfiniteness (e.g., via assumptions about the case-deficiency of nonfinite domains). Two examples are given in the following. Example (18a) shows finite control in Amharic, where the prospective aspectual marker *li-* introduces an irrealis complement; the embedded verb is imperfective and fully inflected (Leung and Halefom 2017: 13). Example (18b) shows finite control in Aromanian,

---

[9] For exposition and implementations of the MTC, see Bowers (1973, 1981), Hornstein (1999, 2003), Boeckx and Hornstein (2003), Boeckx and Hornstein (2004, 2006a,b, 2007), Rodrigues (2004, 2007), Alboiu (2007), Pires (2007), Ferreira (2009), Boeckx et al. (2010a, 2010b), Hornstein and Polinsky (2010), and Martins and Nunes (2017).

[10] For critiques of the MTC, see Culicover and Jackendoff (2001, 2006), Landau (2003, 2007), Kiss (2004), Runner (2006), Rooryck (2007), Barbosa (2009), Bobaljik and Landau (2009), Modesto (2010, 2018), Sato (2011), Ndayiragije (2012), Wood (2012), and Satik (2019).

[11] For exposition and implementations of the Agree-based approach, see Landau (2000, 2004), Adler (2006), Bondaruk (2006), Ussery (2008), Sheehan (2012, 2018b), McFadden (2014), Douglas (2018), Fischer (2018), McFadden and Sundaresan (2018), and Fischer and Flaate Høyem (2022).

where the complementizer *ta* introduces a complement hosting the subjunctive particle *s(i)* and an inflected verb (Manzini and Savoia 2018: 239).

(18) a. käbbädä l-i-bärr-Ø   märrät'ä-Ø.   (*Amharic*)
       Kebede CM-3S.MS-fly.IMP-3SG.M prefer.PERF−3SG.M
       "Kebede preferred to fly."

    b. am   uʁitə   ta   s   u   vɛd.   (*Aromanian*)
       have.1SG   started   that   PRT   it   see.1SG
       "I began to see it."

The most immediate outcome of the Agree-based theory is that PRO must *formally agree* with the controller, a fact that is, surprisingly, not easy to capture under purely semantic conceptions of OC; see (63) and extensive discussion in Landau (2016b, 2018).

There is, however, one empirical effect that falls out naturally from the Agree-based analysis of Landau (2000, 2004) but not under any alternative; it involves the so-called "Visser's generalization," which restricts OC by implicit passive agents (Landau 2000: 169–179). As van Urk (2013) shows, the true generalization is about the interaction of implicit control and agreement.

(19) *Revised Visser's generalization (RVG)*
     Implicit subjects cannot control if T agrees with a referential DP.

In other words, implicit subjects of impersonal passives are free of the RVG. The contrast is illustrated in (20) for Norwegian; van Urk shows that it also holds in German, Dutch, Swedish, Icelandic, and English (the latter allowing less opportunity to observe the RVG due to its unproductive usage of impersonal passives).

(20) a. *Jeg   ble   lovet   å   gi   meg   gaver.
       I   was   promised   COMP   give.INF   me.ACC   gifts
       (Lit.) "I was promised to give me gifts."

    b. Det   ble   lovet   å   gi   meg   gaver.
       there   was   promised   COMP   give.INF   me.ACC   gifts
       (Lit.) "It was promised to give me gifts."

Note that RVG is not about morphological agreement; the forms *ble* "was" in (20a) and (20b) are identical. Nor is it about A-movement; van Urk cites sentences parallel to (20a), except that the matrix object remains in situ (in German and Icelandic), and they are equally ungrammatical. Thus, it is the formation of a *syntactic Agree relation* between a referential DP and T that somehow obstructs implicit OC.

van Urk reasons that RVG reflects the key role of the operation Agree is mediating OC. Following Landau (2000, 2004) (and *unlike* later executions, such as Fischer 2018 and McFadden and Sundaresan 2018), he assumes that a matrix functional head mediates OC. Thus, subject control is established between the matrix subject and PRO because both Agree with T, resulting in feature sharing; object control works the same, via light v. Thus, if T is unavailable to Agree with the controller, OC fails.

van Urk further assumes that the implicit subject of passive is represented in [Spec,vP] as a syntactic D head denoting an existential quantifier, call it $D_\exists$. In impersonal passives (20b), T agrees both with this $D_\exists$ and with PRO, success-fully resulting in implicit subject control. In personal passives (20a), however, T agrees with the matrix goal argument, and thus control by the implicit subject is rendered impossible.[12] The reason why T must Agree with the overt goal DP and not with $D_\exists$ is that only the former requires case-licensing, and case-licensing is parasitic on φ-Agree.

Note that the RVG only specifies when implicit arguments *cannot* control; it does not specify when they *can*. It therefore makes no prediction that OC will succeed in *all* impersonal passives. Indeed, impersonal passives of implicative verbs resist OC in many languages, for reasons independent of agreement (see the discussion of (64b)).

Currently, the RVG is only explainable on the Agree-based theory of OC and not on alternative theories, specifically on the version of that theory that depends on the mediating role of T in subject control. Before closing, let me point out two empirical challenges to the RVG – one that turns out to be spurious, the other one real. Consider first implicit subject control into adjuncts, which is not blocked by agreement with a matrix argument.

(21)   a.   A shed was built to store the tools in.
       b.   The game was played wearing no shoes.
       c.   The president was elected without considering his competence.

These examples are problematic to the RVG only if they instantiate OC by Agree. However, implicit agent control into adjuncts is an instance of NOC, as shown in Landau (2017, 2021a). This is relatively easy to see in (21a), where the storer need not be the builder, but the point is more general and can be demonstrated for other types of adjuncts, using and manipulating the kind of contextual information to which NOC is sensitive, as shown in the works cited.

The other counterexample to RVG is real; it involves implicit subject control into interrogative complements as in (22a).

---

[12] Successful feature sharing (via Agree) between the controller and PRO does not yet guarantee a semantically felicitous result. For goal-control to be possible with *promise*, PRO must be construed as a recipient of permission (e.g., *John was promised to be allowed to watch the movie*); see Landau (2013: 136–148) for extensive discussion of control shift.

(22) a. Mary was asked where to throw the trash.
      b. Ben$_i$ knew that Mary was asked by Sue$_j$ where [PRO$_{*i/j}$ to throw the trash].
      c. *Mary was asked by Ben$_i$ when to call him$_i$.
          [cf. Mary was asked by Ben$_i$ when people should call him$_i$]
      d. *Mary was asked how to improve myself.

Examples (22b)–(22d) serve to demonstrate that interrogative complements under passive verbs instantiate OC and not NOC, thus blocking long-distance, arbitrary, and deictic control, respectively.[13] Given this, (22a) is a genuine exception to the RVG and the contrast between it and (20a) remains a puzzle.

Like other syntactic approaches to OC, the Agree-based account is not free of problems. A fundamental issue, which receives no satisfactory answer, is the distribution of PRO. In the Agree model, PRO is specified [–R], which in turn can only be checked by defective T heads – lacking either semantic tense or morphological agreement. This captures a surface correlation (roughly, the aversion of indicative clauses to PRO) but is little more than a formal redescription of the problem. A second problem concerns the treatment of oblique controllers, which are quite common (e.g., *It is incumbent [upon them] to cooperate with the police*). Oblique arguments are almost universally inert for external agreement, yet they must be visible to the alleged OC-creating Agree operation – even when they cannot trigger agreement on any functional head.

In sum: OC cannot be fully explained by strictly syntactic theories, since they leave too many issues unanswered – from the lexical aspects of controller choice to atypical locality or agreement conditions (unmatched in standard instances of Move and Agree). Nonetheless, the thorough studies of OC within syntactic frameworks have uncovered a wealth of cross-linguistic data to be reckoned with in any comprehensive theory of OC. Importantly, these data establish beyond reasonable doubt that OC *does* implicate a syntactic dependency of some sort, no matter what other types of grammatical machinery it incorporates.

3.2 Lexical-Semantic Theories

Starting from the early 1970s, an alternative to the syntactic account of OC has developed, in which the crucial information used to establish the control relation is lexical and not syntactic. In this research tradition, control rules make reference to thematic roles, thematic hierarchies, semantic classes, and other semantic notions derivable from the lexical content of the control predicate

---

[13] See Landau (2013: 159–160) for further evidence that interrogative complements fall under OC (contrary to what much of the earlier literature assumed). For a different view that classifies them with NOC, see Reed (2018), and for a critique of Reed's data (supporting the OC analysis), see Pitteroff and Schäfer (2019).

(Jackendoff 1974, Chierchia 1984, Nishigauchi 1984, Xu 1986, Sag and Pollard 1991, Růžička 1999, Rooryck 2000, 2007, Jackendoff and Culicover 2003).

Basic observations about the choice of controller motivate a lexical ingredient in any adequate account of OC.

(23) a. Diane$_i$ promised/pledged to Mark$_j$ [PRO$_{i/*j}$ to give a hand].
     b. Diane$_i$ persuaded/encouraged Mark$_j$ [PRO$_{*i/j}$ to give a hand].

(24) a. The promise that was given by Diane$_i$ to Mark$_j$ [PRO$_{i/*j}$ to give a hand].
     b. Mark$_j$ was encouraged [PRO$_j$ to give a hand].

(25) a. Diane$_i$ asked/begged/said to/shouted to Mark$_j$ [PRO$_{*i/j}$ to give a hand].
     b. Diane$_i$ asked/begged [PRO$_{i/*j}$ to give a hand].
     c. Diane$_i$ said/shouted [PRO$_{*i/j}$ to give a hand].

Verbs with similar meanings tend to select the same argument as a controller. Thus, verbs of commitment select the source of the commitment as a controller (23a), while verbs of influence select the target of influence as the controller (23b). These roles are identified thematically and not by any syntactic position, as seen in (24). That distance (or the MDP) cannot fully address these issues is further shown in (25): While some verbs switch from object control to subject control when their object is dropped (or implicit) (25b), others resist this shift and retain the interpretation of control by the (implicit) object (25c). Once again, the relevant verb classes are semantically defined.

Throughout the years, it has proven extremely difficult to pinpoint the semantic components that determine the choice of controller. The main problem with lexicalist accounts is that the analytic categories are either vague or just approximate, with too many cases listed as "exceptions." For example, Chierchia's (1984) thematic hierarchy Theme > Source > Goal > . . . correctly predicts subject (= source) control with *promise*, but wrongly predicts it with other communication verbs like *tell*, *order*, and *require*, which must be labeled as "marked." Sag and Pollard (1991) lump all object control verbs under the category *influence*, even though the object controller of communication verbs is not influenced (e.g., observe the test *What Mary did to John was force/*tell him to clean up his room*).

Jackendoff and Culicover (2003) classify control predicates by underlying "conceptual predicates" (e.g., INTEND, OBLIGATED, REQUEST, etc.), arguing that OC is established at Conceptual Structure (CS) between a designated argument of the conceptual predicate and the embedded subject. Appeal to hidden CS predicates is problematic insofar as speakers have no direct intuitions about the meanings of these predicates; speakers can evaluate what *intend* means but not what the hypothetical INTEND does. Such explanations thus risk circularity (see Boeckx et al. 2010b: 230–237 and Landau 2013: 135–136 for detailed critiques).[14]

A fundamental shortcoming of all purely lexical theories of OC is their inability to identify the controllee position. That position can only be defined *syntactically*, as the embedded *subject*, which may bear any thematic role whatsoever (see Landau 2010: 363, fn. 4).

(26) a. John planned [PRO to work harder].   PRO = agent
      b. John planned [PRO to be a TV host].   PRO = stative bearer of property
      c. John avoided [PRO receiving mail].   PRO = goal
      d. John remembered [PRO fearing ghosts].   PRO = experiencer
      e. John tried [PRO to be elected].   PRO = patient

Now, lexicalist theories might analyze some of these cases with hidden coercion, restoring an invariant, embedded thematic role as the target of control; but that would still beg the question of why that hypothetical role must be realized as the syntactic subject of the complement. The problem is compounded in those lexicalist theories that deny the existence of a syntactic null subject and must therefore reintroduce subjecthood into the lexicon.[15]

Coercion is commonly invoked to explain control shift from subject to object or vice versa, as in *be-allowed-to* complements. Thus, a canonical subject control verb like *promise* shifts to object control and a canonical object control verb like *ask* shifts to subject control.

(27) a. She promised him$_i$ [PRO$_i$ to be allowed to take a picture of himself].
      b. He$_i$ asked her [PRO$_i$ to be allowed to take a picture of himself].

The phenomenon of control shift has been documented early on (Rosenbaum 1967: 92, fn. 13) and received numerous treatments; see Landau (2013: 136–148) for discussion and appraisal of the different proposals. One evident implication of control shift is that the lexical semantics of the control predicate *alone* is not sufficient to determine the controller. Thus, control shift is facilitated by deagentivized and in particular by modalized complements, where PRO is construed as the recipient of permission. Unfortunately, thematic concepts like "causative" of "beneficiary," which figure in some of the lexicalist accounts, are too coarse to pick out this specific flavor of control shift complements (see Uegaki 2011 for an attempt to formally model control shift).

---

[14] Boeckx et al. (2010a) also point out weaknesses in Jackendoff and Culicover's operation of "causative coercion," invoked to explain control shift, to which we presently turn.

[15] See Brame (1976), Bresnan (1978), Bach (1979), Chierchia (1984), Dowty (1985), Culicover and Wilkins (1986), Jacobson (1992), Manzini and Roussou (2000), and Jackendoff and Culicover (2003).

More fundamentally, because both the matrix and the embedded predicate contribute to the acceptability of control shift, lexicalist accounts are led to posit cross-clausal lexical dependencies. This runs counter to the basic idea that lexical relations are strictly local (i.e., spanning a single argument structure). Of course, one can abandon this idea, as is done within HPSG and the Parallel Architecture of Jackendoff, but that would rob the debate about whether OC is to be handled in the syntax or in the lexicon of much of its interest; a lexicon rich enough to express cross-clausal dependencies is for all practical purposes already "syntactic."

A more pressing concern is that control shift appears to be sensitive not only to strictly lexical information but also to the pragmatics of the reported event. Thus, in many languages, an explicit modal is not necessary in the complement, as long as modality is somehow understood from the surrounding context. A helpful hint comes from authority relations between the two participants. Consider sentence (28a) in Hebrew. Out of the blue, it is ambiguous. Whether the object control interpretation (28b) or the subject control one is intended (28c) is entirely up to the context. If we know that the male has authority over the female, we select the former, and if we know that it is the female who has authority over the male, we select the latter interpretation.

(28) a. hu$_i$ bikeš   mimena$_j$ [PRO$_{i/j}$ le'hiša'er].
          he   asked   from.her   to.stay
      b. He requested from her that she would stay.
      c. He asked for her permission to stay.

The understanding that pragmatics has an important role in choosing the controller in OC – even if syntax has a decisive role in delimiting the domain in which it must occur, in accordance with the OC signature – has first made its entrance to control studies in Farkas (1988). Farkas introduced the semantic notion *Responsibility*: RESP(i,s) holds between an initiator i and a situation s just in case i intentionally brings about s. In the unmarked case, like (23a) and (23b), the controller of an infinitive describing situation s is just the matrix argument that is the initiator of s. In control shift situations, such as (27), the controller is the individual whose actions are determined by the initiator.

While RESP in Farkas' analysis, unfortunately, is an intuitive rather than a formalized concept, it transcends the limits of strictly lexicalist accounts by explicitly incorporating pragmatic considerations. The concept of "initiator" is broader than "agent," and applies to secondary agents of passives (e.g., *King was deliberately arrested*) as well as to NOC by extra-sentential antecedents (e.g., *The shop window has a big sale sign in it in order to attract customers*). The RESP relation is not reducible to thematic roles, and has a "global" character in that it is sensitive both to the matrix and the embedded eventuality. In these respects, it can be thought of a precursor of the ESA theories to be discussed in the next subsection.

Last to be mentioned within the lexicalist camp are recent attempts to model the semantics of OC using the formal apparatus of attitude reports (Stephenson 2010, Pearson 2013, 2016, 2018). These accounts are lexicalist insofar as they derive the OC dependency from the lexical denotation of the control predicate; however, that should not imply that they deny the existence of PRO (normally they acknowledge it) or the importance of syntax in feeding compositional semantics with the right structures for interpretation. Commonly in these accounts, a λ-abstractor is inserted at the edge of the complement, binding PRO and yielding a property denotation. This property serves as the first argument of the control verb, which, being an attitude predicate, quantifies over structured worlds/contexts, for example, over tuples of <individual,world,time>. It is the lexical meaning of this predicate that asserts the control implication; namely, that in each of these contexts, the complement property holds of the doxastic counterpart of the attitude holder (e.g., subject control with *want*) or of its addressee (e.g., object control with *tell*). The notion of "doxastic counterpart" encodes self-identification, accounting for the obligatory *de se* reading of PRO in attitude complements.

The biggest advantage of formal semantic analyses of OC is their explicitness; one can track exactly how the meaning of an OC construction is composed from the meaning of its parts. However, these analyses leave a few major questions unanswered.

First, the syntactic relation between the controller and PRO is lost, since PRO is locally bound by an operator, which bears no syntactic relation to the controller. This leaves unexplained the basic fact of agreement – PRO must agree with the controller, even in cases where the agreement is merely formal; see (63), Landau (2016b), and especially Landau (2018). Second, the formal semantic accounts do not really address the hard question of controller choice: What makes certain verbs cluster together and differently from other verbs with respect to subject or object control? Specifying in the lexical entry of each control verb the "designated argument," whose doxastic counterpart is identified with the individual coordinate of the world-time-individual triplet quantified over by the predicate, misses obvious generalizations that cut across OC verbs.[16] Furthermore, we have seen that the relevant generalizations are sensitive to variable pragmatic information, which cannot be specified in lexical entries. Finally, the basic assumption that OC complements *uniformly* denote

---

[16] See Mucha and Hartmann (2022) for initial experimental results from German on the availability of control shift vis à vis the attitude/nonattitude distinction and the (embedded) active/passive distinction.

properties is at odds with a number of distinctions that naturally fall out of a systematic cut between property complements and propositional complements (see Section 5 on the dual analysis of control).

In sum, lexicalist accounts of OC have made important contributions to our understanding that OC is not a "blind" syntactic dependency between two positions like, for example, A-movement, which is oblivious to the semantic roles of the related positions. The semantic roles, as well as the overall construal of causal and deontic relations that tie together the matrix and the embedded eventualities, all conspire to determine which matrix argument is selected as the controller. Lexical entries cannot encode every aspect of these construals, but they certainly *restrict* the range of construals available in control constructions and, correspondingly, the choice of controller.

3.3 Embedded Speech Act Theories

While lexicalist theories focus their attention on the argument structure of the control verb and try to formulate systematic correlations between thematic roles and controller choice, ESA theories highlight the type of speech act – by which we include both actual speech acts and mental "acts" such as decisions, plans, and so on – expressed by the OC complement. The leading idea behind this approach is that the choice of controller naturally falls out from the proper identification of this speech act, using a couple of systematic "bridging" principles. These bridging principles make crucial reference to indexical information tagged on the participants in the speech event.

One can discern two strands of research converging on ESA theories. The first strand was launched in Postal (1970), specifically in the appendix to that study, and was gradually developed, syntactically and semantically, in Kuno (1972), Bianchi (2003), Schlenker (2003, 2011), Anand and Nevins (2004), Anand (2006), Baker (2008), Stephenson (2010), Landau (2015, 2018), and Stegovec (2019). The second strand has been developed within studies of OC in East Asian languages, mostly Japanese and Korean. Curiously, these two strands have evolved quite independently of each other, although they reach very similar conclusions. I will start by describing Postal's original idea and then proceed directly to the literature on East Asian languages, which provides striking support for it.

Postal (1970) made three key observations regarding the relation between OC and ESAs. First, infinitival OC complements often have a finite counterpart with a characteristic modal. Second, the understood controller of the silent subject of the infinitive (later called PRO) corresponds to the understood antecedent of the subject pronoun in the modal finite counterpart; see the pairs (a)–(b) in (29)–(32). Third, there is a systematic correlation between the choice of matrix subject or matrix object antecedent of the pronominal subject in the Indirect Discourse (ID) complements in the (b) examples and a first or second pronoun in their Direct Discourse (DD) counterparts in the (c) examples.

(29) a. Harry told Betty$_i$ PRO$_i$ to marry him.
      b. Harry told Betty$_i$ that she$_i$ should marry him.
      c. (**You**) marry me, Harry told Betty.

(30) a. Harry asked Betty$_i$ PRO$_i$ to marry him.
      b. Harry asked Betty$_i$ if she$_i$ would marry him.
      c. Will **you** (please) marry me, Harry asked Betty.

(31) a. Harry$_i$ promised Betty PRO$_i$ to leave.
      b. Harry$_i$ promised Betty that he$_i$ would leave.
      c. **I** will leave, Harry promised Mary.

(32) a. Harry$_i$ asked Betty when PRO$_i$ to leave.
      b. Harry$_i$ asked Betty when he$_i$ should leave.
      c. When should **I** leave, Harry asked Betty.

The emerging generalization, which Postal stated, was this.

(33) *Generalization*: If the DD subject is second person, the ID subject (PRO) is object-controlled; if the DD subject is first person, the ID subject is subject-controlled.

Note that Postal's reference to *modality* would more accurately be described today as *mood*, that is, illocutionary force. It is the parallelism between the *force* of the complements in the (a)–(b) pairs that is tied to the choice of antecedent: For example, the subject of the content of a promise is identified with the promiser (Speaker), while the subject of the content of a directive is identified with the one being directed (Addressee). Deontic modality here is a concomitant feature of speech acts imposing commitments on either the speaker or the addressee.

As to the most interesting question of why controller choice would correlate with the *person* feature of a DD counterpart, Postal had the following to say (p. 496): "If Fact C [generalization (33), *IL*], which represents a correlation between properties of 'corresponding' Direct and Indirect Discourse sentences, is to provide an explanation for the operation of EQUI in Indirect Discourse sentences, it must be the case that underlying structures of such Indirect Discourse sentences manifest properties somehow linked to the surface properties of the relevant Direct Discourse sentences."

In other words, underlying PRO there must be some "ancestor" with properties "somehow linked" to the indexical pronouns that figure in the DD paraphrases. While current theory no longer relates ID and DD (or finite and nonfinite clauses) transformationally, Postal's insight is conceptually independent of such derivations.

At its core, it amounts to the appealing idea that in those complements that paraphrase ESA, OC PRO is interpreted as if it were an indexical pronoun. This insight has proven very fruitful in subsequent work on OC. In particular, it finds interesting support in the grammatical expression of OC in East Asian languages.[17]

The Japanese/Korean scholarship on OC as ESA capitalizes on two observations: (i) In matrix clauses, certain mood particles restrict their subject to first person, second person, or inclusive plural first person ("I+you"); (ii) in embedded clauses, the very same mood particles restrict the choice of controller to the matrix speaker/author, addressee, or their combination.

Starting with (i), a first person subject is selected by the promissive (PRM), intentive (INT), and optative (OPT) mood markers; second person is selected by the imperative (IMP) mood marker; and inclusive first plural person subject is selected by the exhortative (EXH) mood marker (Japanese data from Matsuda 2021: 147–148).[18]

(34) a. Watasi/Watasitati/??Anata/??Anatatati/??Kare/??Karera}-wa hatiji-ni kaer-**u**.
        I/We/??You/??You.PL/??He/??They-TOP   eight-at   go.home-**PRM**
        "I'll/We'll go home at eight."

     b. *Watasi/*Watasitati/Omae/Omaetati/*Kare/*Karera-wa hayakuronbun kak-**e**!
        *I/*We/You/You.PL/*He/*They-TOP   soon paper write-**IMP**
        "(You) write that paper soon!"

     c. Watasitati/??Anatatati/*Karera-wa shukudai si-**yoo**.
        We/??You.PL/*They-TOP   homework do-**EXH**
        "Why don't we do our homework." / "Let's do our homework."

To my knowledge, it was Pak et al. (2008) and Madigan (2008a, 2008b) who first proposed to connect between observations (i) and (ii) and derive the choice of controller from the choice of the mood marker on the embedded clause, in other words, from the type of speech act embedded under the control verb, which is exactly Postal's (1970) original insight. This idea has been put to use, in various forms, in Lee (2009), Seo and Hoe (2015), Sisovics (2018), Matsuda (2019, 2021), and Liao and Wang (2022).[19]

As Lee and Madigan observed, there must be some fit between the matrix verb and the embedded mood markers. A verb like *order* cannot embed a promise and a verb like *promise* cannot embed a directive. Nonetheless,

---

[17] To streamline this idea with the upcoming analysis in Section 5.1, we can reinterpret PRO in these studies as the "perspectival *pro*" in Spec,CP (Landau 2015, 2018, 2020). PRO itself is merely a λ-abstractor; the locus of the indexical information is *pro*.

[18] The actual person feature of the subject need not always match its overt form, which is why some of the "mismatched" options in (34) are not totally excluded. Such "hidden" person features are familiar from the study of imperatives (e.g., *Everyone wash yourselves!*); see Zanuttini (2008).

[19] See Hasegawa (2009), Stegovec (2019), and Burukina (2023) for interesting extensions of the same framework.

many verbs are somewhat flexible and allow more than one choice. It is here that the effect of the mood marker is most striking. The examples in (35) show how the choice of the embedded mood marker determines the control options under the Korean verb *mal* "say" (Madigan 2008b: 167, 174).

(35) a. Inho₁-ka   Hwun₂-eykey *pro*₁/₂/₃   swuyeng-ha-n-ta-ko   mal-ha-yess-ta.
Inho-NOM   Hwun-DAT   swim-do-IND-DC-C   tell-do-PST-DC
"Inho₁ told Hwun₂ that he₁/she₂/someone₃ is swimming."

b. Inho₁-ka   Hwun₂-eykey PRO*₁/₂/*₃   swuyeng-ha-**keyss**-ta-ko
Inho-NOM   Hwun-DAT   swim-**VOL**-DC-C
mal-ha-yess-ta.
tell-do-PST-DC
"Inho₁ said to Hwun₂ that he₁/*she₂/*someone would swim."

c. Inho₁-ka   Hwun₂-eykey PRO*₁/ ₂/*₃ swuyeng-ha-**la**-ko   mal-ha-yess-ta.
Inho-NOM   Hwun-DAT   swim-do-**IMP**-C   tell-do-PST-DC
"Inho told Hwun to swim."

d. Inho₁-ka   Hwun₂-eykey PRO₁ ₊₂/*₁/*₂/*₃ swuyeng-ha-**ca**-ko   mal-ha-yess-ta.
Inho-NOM   Hwun-DAT   swim-do-**EXH**-C   tell-do-PST-DC
"Inho₁ said to Hwun₂ that they₁₊₂/*₃ should go swimming."

The indicative present tense marker *(n)un-ta* does not induce control (35a); the volitional marker *keyss*, which is speaker-oriented in matrix clauses, induces subject control in complements (35b); the imperative marker *la*, which is addressee-oriented in matrix clauses, induces object control in complements (35c); and the exhortative marker *ca*, which is oriented to the speaker + addressee in matrix clauses, induces split control in complements (35d).

Consider now how this causal relation between the mood marker and controller choice is cashed out in the relevant studies. In Pak et al. 2008, promises, directives, and so on are expressed by *jussive* clauses, which essentially contribute properties to the "To-Do List" of the speaker/ addressee. Mood markers are functional heads projecting a JussP, establishing agreement with the local DP (= subject) and endowing it with interpretable person features, interpreted as referential presuppositions. They also introduce a λ-binder to bind the subject variable and produce the property added to the To-Do List (Zanuttini et al. 2012).

In embedded contexts, the speaker/addressee participant is shifted to the reported speech (or thought) event. If c^* is the utterance context and c' is the reported context, then Speaker(c') and Addressee(c') will pick out the subject and object of the matrix verb, respectively. This is achieved by context shift, in analogy to treatments of indexical shift, where the attitude verb is taken to quantify over contexts, for example, tuples of <world, time, speaker, addressee> (Schlenker 2003). Pak et al. (2008) and Madigan (2008a) make direct reference to [person] as the key feature identifying the matrix controller, whereas Madigan (2008b) uses thematic roles like Agent to do so. However, both assume that PRO is, in essence, a shifted indexical.

The ESA theory of OC is appealing in a number of ways and seems particularly suitable for East Asian languages. It is predicated on a very natural intuition – namely, that (attitude) OC verbs are just an instance of verbs introducing ID; that this discourse typically involves deontic commitments to bring about a certain state of affairs; and that the identity of the party entrusted with bringing it about is systematically correlated with, and predictable from, the type of thought or speech act involved (intention, promise, directive, exhortation, etc.). Finally, it offers a natural account of the *de se* reading characteristic of PRO in attitude complements; it is essentially reduced to the obligatory *de se* reading associated with first person indexicals.[20]

One general puzzle about OC that may receive a principled explanation within the ESA theory is the existence of PC (Wilkinson 1971, Landau 2000, 2004, 2016b, Sheehan 2012, 2014, 2018a,b, White and Grano 2014, Pearson 2016, Grano 2017a, Pitterofff et al. 2017, Authier and Reed 2018, 2020, Pitteroff and Sheehan 2018). In genuine PC, the referential relation between the controller and the controllee is a subset relation, rather than identity (the latter is the case only in "fake PC"; see Pitterofff et al. 2017, Pitteroff and Sheehan 2018). The "residue," uncontrolled part is picked up from salient antecedents (in discourse or in the conversational context; a PC construal is notated as index "i+" on PRO).

(36) We thought that . . .
    a. The chair$_i$ preferred [PRO$_{i+}$ to gather at 6].
    b. Bill$_i$ regretted [PRO$_{i+}$ meeting without a concrete agenda].
    c. Mary$_i$ wondered [whether PRO$_{i+}$ to apply together for the grant].
    d. It was humiliating to the chair$_i$ [PRO$_{i+}$ to disperse so abruptly].

PC is attested in complements of attitude predicates; thus, it is not available, for example, in implicative complements (37a). Furthermore, the plurality of PRO under PC is of a rather abstract nature, resisting morphological plural marking as well as distributive readings (37b)–(37c) (Landau 2016a,b, Authier and Reed 2018, 2020), at least in most languages.

(37) a. * (We thought that) John$_i$ managed [PRO$_{i+}$ to gather at 6].
    b. * (We thought that) the chair$_i$ preferred [PRO$_{i+}$ to work as partners].
    c. (We thought that) Helen wanted [PRO$_{i+}$ to (*each) answer a different question].

---

[20] More precisely, both first person pronouns and subject-controlled PRO are interpreted via a semantic predicate that picks out a self-identifying participant, namely Speaker/Author(c), producing a *de se* reading; and both second person pronouns and object-controlled PRO are interpreted via a semantic predicate that picks out a participant identified as an addressee, namely Addressee(c).

There is a great deal more to say about PC; recent research has documented restricted deviations from the generalizations exemplified in (37) in various languages, which space limitations prevent us from discussing (see Landau 2024). Nevertheless, these core properties hold across many languages and constructions to warrant a principled explanation.

While PC can be modeled in many different ways – via syntactic agreement, lexical entailments, or pragmatic implicatures – many of these ways remain descriptive. A true insight appeared in Matsuda (2019, 2021), where a link between PC and the associative semantics of indexical pronouns was proposed. Matsuda's account proceeds in two steps. First, it is noted that the standard semantics of [person] is associative; thus, *we* means "a group including the speaker" and *you*$_{PL}$ means "a group including the addressee" (rather than "speakers" and "addressees"); See Noyer 1992, Cysouw 2003, Bobaljik 2008, and Wechsler 2019. Indeed, this is how indexical features are interpreted within the presuppositional approach to φ-features (Heim 2008, Kratzer 2009):

(38) a. $[\text{AUTHOR}]^{g,c} = \lambda x_e{:}x$ includes the speaker/thinker in c.x.
       b. $[\text{ADDRESSEE}]^{g,c} = \lambda x_e{:}x$ includes the addressee in c.x.

Second, following the ESA theory, OC PRO is essentially an indexical pronoun – first person in subject control and second person in object control. Thus, the associative semantics is available *by default* to OC PRO in attitude contexts (reported speech or thought) and requires no special amendments.

Nonetheless, as pointed out in Landau (2015: 35–37), a full reduction of OC PRO to shifted indexicals still faces significant difficulties. First, the distribution of shifted indexicals is very different from that of OC PRO, being restricted to a handful of verbs (often no more than three), in contexts of indicative (uncontrolled) complements, often distinguishing between first and second person pronouns, and so on, not to mention that OC is by far more common than indexical shift. Perhaps the most immediate challenge to this theory is the fact that unlike shifted indexicals, OC PRO conceals its indexical character and inherits its morphological [person] value from the controller (as indicated on agreeing elements).

(39) a. John planned [PRO$_{[pers:3]}$ to promote himself/*myself].
       b. John planned: "I will promote myself."

As Landau (2015: 37) observes,

> This mismatch between the form and semantic value of OC PRO in attitude contexts is ... particularly thorny for the indexical shift theory, since on this theory, PRO is *inherently specified* as the context's author or addressee, just as the pronouns *I* and *you* are. To reconcile these facts, one would have to

maintain that only in the case of shifted indexicals (but not in the case of unshifted ones) are [person] features semantically interpreted but morphologically unspecified, and that a separate process of agreement (with the controller) guarantees their morphological valuation.

Indeed, recognizing the agreement problem in the analysis of Korean OC, Seo and Hoe (2015) go as far as proposing that despite appearances, OC complements are not embedded jussive clauses but rather embedded subjunctive clauses whose heads do not encode indexical information.

The morphological features of PRO present a genuine problem for ESA theories of OC, which persists in more sophisticated implementations, like Matsuda (2019, 2021). As the authors before her, Matsuda assumes that OC complements are evaluated against a shifted context. However, in her account, PRO is not a minimal pronoun, but rather intrinsically valued for participant features – [+SP,–AD] for speaker, [–SP,+AD] for addressee, and [+SP,+AD] for inclusive speaker. These are crucially semantic features, anchored to a given context, as distinct from morphological person features. Matsuda proposes that when anchored to the utterance context, these features yield an overt pronoun with first or second person morphology. However, when anchored to the shifted context, they yield a controlled null third person subject – that is, PRO.

Distributional and typological issues that face the reduction of PRO to shifted indexicals face this proposal too. In addition, because it rejects the minimal pronoun analysis, Matsuda's account is committed to a three-way *lexical* distinction between three types of PRO: a first person PRO for speaker control, a second person PRO for addressee control, and a person-less PRO for non-attitude control.

While the anchoring of the pronoun's interpretation to context is semantically natural, the anchoring of its *spellout* to context leaves open the question of why null PRO cannot occur in embedded object positions. In Matsuda (2019: 109), this is attributed to agreement with T, governed by locality. However, Matsuda (2021) discards this idea, presumably to avoid positing a [tense] feature on PRO. This overgenerates pronouns specified, for example, $[+SP_c,-AD_c]$ (with c the reported context) even in embedded object positions. Finally, the possibility of first/second person PRO becomes a problem, especially when they are misaligned with the [SP]/[AD] coordinates of the utterance context.

(40)   a.   You decided [PRO to harm yourself].
           Controller: $[-SP_{c*},+AD_{c*}]$; PRO: $[+SP_{c'},-AD_{c'}]$
       b.   You urged me [PRO to harm myself].
           Controller: $[+SP_{c*},-AD_{c*}]$; PRO: $[-SP_{c'},+AD_{c'}]$

Here, it seems that PRO *morphologically* agrees with the controller. However, because her spellout rules cannot generate first/second person on PRO, Matsuda is led to suggest that PRO is *always* third person, even in (40a) and (40b), and that the reflexives agree directly with the controller. This, however, runs counter to standard conceptions of agreement and binding, and (as Matsuda 2019: 192 admits) cannot explain why the same agreement facts hold when the reflexive is read *de se*, namely, on its natural reading, where it is semantically bound by PRO.[21]

Overall, then, ESA theories of OC offer an insightful treatment of the *de se* interpretation, of the occurrence of mood markers in OC complements, of controller choice, and of the existence of PC. However, they still grapple with the morphological agreement properties of OC PRO.

4 Nonobligatory Control

OC clauses display a characteristic internal morphosyntax. In most languages, an OC clause is nonfinite and its subject is null. However, we have also seen cases where the OC clause is finite and cases where its subject is overt (Section 3.1). Whichever shape OC clauses take in a given language, their external distribution is severely limited; they only display OC in very specific environments. When they occur elsewhere, we observe NOC. In other words, NOC is how we designate the non-OC behavior of clauses that *can* display OC in principle. Clauses that never display OC to begin with, for example, finite clauses in most languages, are perforce not eligible to NOC; their uncontrolled behavior is more transparently described as no control (NC), even when harboring a null subject. As we will see in what follows, the interpretive profile of NOC PRO is more restricted than just any pronoun, including *pro*.

To illustrate, Spanish infinitives display OC in complement position (41a), but finite complements display NC (41c). Correspondingly, the former display NOC in subject position (41b) and the latter maintain their NC character there (41d).

(41) a. Juan$_i$ quería [PRO$_{i/*j}$ comprar]. un caballo OC
          Juan wanted   to.buy   a horse
          "Juan wanted to buy a horse."
      b. [PRO comprar un caballo] sería.   un error   *NOC*
               to.buy a horse   would.be   an error
          "To buy a horse would be an error."

---

[21] On the challenges that *de re* reflexives pose to theories of agreement and binding, see Heim (1994) and Sharvit (2011). See Landau (2018) on the specific problem they pose for property-based theories of OC and Pearson (2018) for a proposal on how to address these problems.

    c. Juan$_i$ recordó [que *pro*$_{i/j}$ había comprado un caballo].   *NC*
       Juan remembered that   had   bought   a horse
       "Juan remembered that he had bought a horse."

    d. [Que *pro* compro un caballo] fue   un error.   *NC*
       that   bought a   horse   was an error
       "That he bought a horse was a mistake."

While the general principles governing the interpretation of *pro* are well worth studying and often overlap those that govern NOC, they will be set aside in the following. With this in mind, we can turn to a descriptive definition of NOC, constructed in opposition to the OC signature in (4).

(42)   *The NOC signature*
      In a control construction [. . . [$_S$ PRO . . .] . . .], if:
      a. The controller need not be a grammatical element, and when it is, need not be a codependent of S, AND
      b. PRO need not be interpreted as a bound variable (i.e., it may be a free variable) then this is an *NOC* construction.

As noted in Landau (2013: 231, fn. 2), studies of NOC have almost exclusively focused on English. This assessment is still largely true, so one should bear in mind that much of what follows has yet to be tested across many more languages.

While OC and NOC tend to align with different syntactic configurations, the alignment is not absolute. Thus, OC is canonically attested in selected complements and in a few types of adjuncts (see Section 5.2 on adjunct control), whereas NOC is canonically attested in subject/extraposed clauses and also in certain types of adjuncts. However, oddballs exist on both sides. Obligatory control into subject clauses is found with evaluative adjectives and *easy*-adjectives (Landau 2013: 41–43). Conversely, NOC is also found in some selected complements, as will be shortly seen.

A variety of NOC examples in English is presented in what follows. Note that the controller of PRO is rather free in these examples, corresponding to one or two long-distance antecedents, a deictic participant, or some arbitrary referent. In the following, we examine these interpretive options more closely.

(43)   *NOC in English*
      a. *Subject clause (super-equi)*
        John$_i$ finally realized that [PRO$_{i+j}$ hurting each other] really bothered Sue$_j$.
      b. *Subject clause (deictic control)*
        Clearly, [PRO confessing my crime] was not something they anticipated.
      c. *Extraposed clause*
        I never understood why it is bad for health [PRO$_{arb}$ to stuff oneself with marshmallows].

d. *Temporal adjunct*
[After PRO pitching the tents], darkness fell quickly.

e. *"Without"-clause*
There will be no progress [without PRO investing economic and human resources].

f. *Infinitival relative*
Is there anywhere [PRO to stay for the night] in this town?

All these examples share the NOC property in (42a) – the controller is not a codependent of the nonfinite clause containing PRO. The same point can be demonstrated using VP-ellipsis. While OC PRO inside in an ellipsis site only admits a sloppy reading, NOC PRO allows a strict reading as well (Nishigauchi 1984, Bouchard 1985), since its controller is not confined to the clause containing the infinitive or gerund.

(44) a. John$_i$ tried [PRO$_i$ to leave early],
and Bill$_j$ did too ~~try [PRO$_{j/*i}$ to leave early]~~.

b. John$_i$ realized that [PRO$_i$ introducing himself] would help everyone, and Mary$_j$ did too ~~realize that [PRO$_{i/j}$ introducing himself/herself] would help everyone~~.

To illustrate property (42b), consider the following pair.

(45) a. *OC (only sloppy reading)*
[Only Bill]$_i$ expects [PRO$_i$ to recite *The Tiger*].

b. *NOC (sloppy or strict reading)*
[Only Bill]$_i$ expected that [[PRO$_i$ reciting *The Tiger*] would impress Jane].

Example (45a) asserts that Bill is the only person X who entertained the expectation that X would recite *The Tiger*. In contrast, (45b) is ambiguous. On the sloppy reading, it asserts that Bill is the only person X who entertained the expectation that X's reciting *The Tiger* would impress Mary. On the strict reading, it asserts that Bill is the only person who entertained the expectation that Bill's reciting *The Tiger* would impress Mary. Thus, if both Bill and Peter, and only them, expected that Bill's reciting *The Tiger* would impress Mary, the sloppy reading of (45b) would be true but the strict reading false.

For a long while, it has been assumed that NOC never occurs in complements (Manzini 1983, Koster 1984, Vanden Wyngaerd 1994, Landau 2000; although see Jackendoff and Culicover 2003 for a dissenting view). In particular, Landau (2013: section 1.6) has argued that all apparent cases of NOC into complements conceal one of two possible complications: Either the true controller is a local implicit argument (hence, this is OC) or the complement is not really a complement of V but is rather embedded inside a nominalization (whose head is null), where the extra intervening structure is responsible for NOC. While these analyses are supported for many if not most of the relevant cases, they cannot fully eliminate NOC into complements. Genuine NOC is attested in complements to communication verbs, as shown in Landau (2020).

Landau (2020) discusses an example of the following kind.

(46)   Dad said [PRO to be quiet].

Here the controller of PRO is not overtly specified. Many authors have taken this property as sufficient grounds for classifying such examples as NOC (Williams 1980, Bresnan 1982, Bouchard 1984, Huang 1989, Sag and Pollard 1991, Dalrymple 2001). However, the relevant interpretations discussed do not really establish NOC, as the reference of PRO is linked to the local implicit goal of *say*. The question is whether this reading exhausts the possibilities. Landau (2020) argues that it does not.

Consider the goal-less appearance of *say* (or similar verbs, like *order, recommend*, etc.) in a richer context.

(47)   Dad is reading in the living room. Jen, his older daughter, is there too, working on the computer. The little boys are in their room, making a hell lot of noise. Dad tells Jen to go tell the kids to be quiet. Jen walks over to the boys' room, enters it and utters:

   "Dad said to be quiet" / "Dad said to behave yourselves."

The intended, perfectly natural reading of (47), cannot be rendered via an implicit controller. The addressee of dad's speech act was Jen, but in the given scenario, (47) does not mean what (48) does.

(48)   Dad said to Jen [PRO to be quiet].

The only reading (48) affords is that dad said to Jen that *she* should be quiet; whereas (47) conveys the proposition that dad said to Jen that *the boys* should be quiet. The fact that PRO can bear the features [2PL], despite the fact that *Jen* bears [3SG], further illustrates that (47) is not reducible to implicit OC.

To accommodate these findings, Landau (2020) proposes that configuration alone does not fully determine the OC/NOC status of a complement, and that finer selectional distinctions are relevant as well. Specifically, the head of OC complements encodes the reported context and PRO may only be anchored to some coordinate of that context (AUTHOR or ADDRESSEE). In NOC clauses, including NOC complements, the C head is unrestricted as to which context it encodes, thus allowing PRO to be anchored to a coordinate of remote or deictic contexts.

Notably missing from the characterization of NOC in (42) is the requirement that PRO be [+human], which has regularly been taken to be definitional of NOC PRO (see Chomsky 1981: 324–327 for the original observations and then much subsequent literature, e.g., Williams 1992, Kawasaki 1993, Moltmann 2006, Landau 2013). It is indeed the case that NOC PRO resists a [−human] interpretation in many contexts that would seem to support it ((49a) and (49b) are from Chomsky 1981: 324, 326; (49c) is from Williams 1992; and (49d) is from Kawasaki 1993: 30).

(49) a. It is possible [PRO$_{arb}$ to roll down the hill].
   [cf. *It is possible for the rocks to roll down the hill*].
   b. * [PRO to snow all day] would be a nuisance.
   [cf. *For it to snow all day would be a nuisance*].
   c. * The open window$_i$ proves that [before PRO$_i$ breaking], it was raining.
   d. # [After PRO$_{arb}$ being spoiled in a refrigerator], there is nothing even a good cook can do.

Nonetheless, recent empirical work on NOC has unearthed naturally occurring data with inanimate NOC PRO; see especially Donaldson (2021: 127–139). These examples are far less frequent than the common [+human] NOC PRO, but they still exist. Example (50a) is a Spanish example from Herbeck (2021: 261); (50b) is from Landau (2021a: 124); and (50c) is from Donaldson (2021: 132).

(50) a. En   Madrid$_i$ la   policía yo creo   que   sí
        in   Madrid   the   police   I   think   that   yes
        que   trabaja   bien [para PRO$_i$ ser   una ciudad grand
        that   work.3SG well for   be.INF   a   city   big
        donde   tienen   más   problemas que   aquí].
        where   have.3PL more problems   than   here
        "In Madrid$_i$ I think that the police does work quite well, taking into account that it is a big city where they have more problems than here."
        (Lit. [PRO$_i$ being a big city ...])
   b. [PRO$_i$ having run smoothly for years], it was finally time for my car$_i$ to be serviced.
   c. Sewage treatment plants do not capture all the beads which wash down the drain, so some$_i$ inevitably end up in the sea. And [PRO$_i$ being so small, no one really knows where they$_i$ are going].

What is the source of this confusion over the [±human] value of NOC PRO? To answer this question, we must take a look at the theoretical approaches to this element.

From the outset, there have been two main approaches to the question of how the reference of NOC PRO is established. One approach holds that NOC PRO is linked to the current sentential *topic* (Bresnan 1982, Kawasaki 1993, Adler 2006, Janke and Bailey 2017, Donaldson 2021); the other approach holds that it is linked to the prominent *logophoric* center (Kuno 1975, Williams 1992,

Landau 2001, Green 2018). That *both* notions are needed to fully account for NOC, and neither is reducible to the other, is proposed in Lyngfelt (2000), hinted in Landau (2013: 255–256), and fully embraced in Landau (2021a) (see also McFadden and Sundaresan 2018). On such a dual approach, cases like (49) would fall under logophoric control and cases like (50) would fall under topic control. Since a logophoric antecedent must harbor some mental perspective, its [+human] character follows at once.[22] In contrast, topical elements may, in principle, be [–human] (we return in what follows to the infelicity of (49b)–(49d)).

Disentangling topicality from logophoricity is a delicate matter. The very notion of a "logophoric center" implies some salience – a discourse may introduce a number of logophoric antecedents (sentient individuals whose mental perspective is involved in the reported situation), but only one or two of them would count as salient enough for the purposes of serving as an antecedent for the logophoric element. This distance effect is well-known from *picture*-logophors, which are, by assumption, exempt from condition A.

(51)   Ann realized that Bob disliked many pictures of himself/*herself.

Since salience plays into both topicality and logophoric antecedence, the two criteria often pick out the same antecedent. To address this confound, Landau (2021a: 126) set up the following paradigm.

(52)   *NOC by [–top,+log] antecedent*
       a. A: What about the certificates of appreciation? What happened to them?
          B: They were handed out before announcing the winners.
       NOC by [+top,–log] antecedent
       b. A: What about Mary? Is she available?
          B: Well, after sneaking outside last night, her father grounded her for a week.

In both cases, utterance A establishes the topic for utterance B. The logophoric center is the implicit agent in (52a) and *her father* in (52b) (the speaker and hearer are always available as topics and logophoric centers). An implicit agent of passive is very low on the accessibility scale (Ariel 1990), certainly compared to the surface subject, and especially compared to a surface subject that is previously established as a topic. Example (52a), then, displays NOC by a logophoric center that is neither a topic from discourse nor from the utterance situation (it need not be the speaker). In (52b), *Mary* is the established topic, but

---

[22] [+human] should be understood in a broad sense, extending to higher animals, complex machines, computers, softwares, etc.; essentially any entity to which it is possible to impute mental states. Philosophical quibbles aside, speakers freely engage in such verbal practices (e.g., *My car hates me, The computer tried to connect to the network but failed*).

not a logophoric center (the patient argument of *ground* bears no mental perspective to the event). Thus, it is a case of NOC by a topic that is not a logophoric center.

Thus, we conclude that topicality and logophoricity are each in itself sufficient for NOC, but neither one is necessary. This is a familiar pattern. Logophoric pronouns in West African languages (Adesola 2005) and long-distance reflexives in East Asian languages (Huang 1994, Han and Storoshenko 2012, Nishigauchi 2014) are also "doubly" licensed, either by logophoricity or by topicality. Whether this consistent duality reflects a purely grammatical system or some general cognitive feature is a question to be addressed by future research.

We now face an empirical puzzle. Granted that the logophoric path requires a [+human] PRO, the topic-oriented path still does not. But if [+human] is not strictly required of topics, why is it that NOC PRO nevertheless so often seems to resist [–human] interpretations (see (49))? Landau (2021a) suggests that topics too are preferentially human, a well-established typological finding (Givón 1976, Comrie 1981, DuBois 1987, Song 2001, Swierskia 2004). Kuno's (2006: 316) notion of Empathy Topic is particularly apt to capture the natural coupling of humanness and topics, positing that "it is more difficult for the speaker to empathize with a non-human animate object than with a human, and more difficult to empathize with an inanimate object than with an animate object."

Thus, topic-oriented referents tend to be human because they attract the speaker's empathy, and the speaker's empathy is impeded by inanimate or nonhuman referent. This makes [+human] a strong default even on the topic-oriented path of NOC. Presumably, this default can be overridden under specific discourse circumstances, such as in (50). No doubt further fine-detailed work is needed to spell out these circumstances and advance our understanding how they arise for different speakers in different languages.[23]

The final kind of NOC involves meteorological and temporal predicates ((53a) is from Quirk et al. 1985: 1122; (53b) is from Kortmann 1991: 50; and (53c) is from Duffley 2014: 181).

(53) a. Being Christmas, the government offices were closed.
      b. Being Sunday, all banks were closed.
      c. Having rained all day long, the hill has become a virtual mud slide.

---

[23] The idea that multiple factors – lexical, syntactic, pragmatic, and processing-related – interact in the ultimate resolution of NOC as well as in determining how accessible different NOC readings are in specific environments is an insight shared by Kortmann (1991), Lyngfelt (2000), Green (2018), Donaldson (2021), Herbeck (2021), and Landau (2021a).

Landau (2021a) suggests that these cases also fall under topic control, adopting Erteschik-Shir's (1997) idea that the subject of these predicates is the spatiotemporal location of the event, a special kind of topic termed "stage topic." When overt, this subject of predication surfaces as a semi-argumental expletive. In contrast, *pure* expletives that fail to denote anything cannot be so used – the so-called repeatedly observed "ban on expletive PRO" ((54a) is adapted from Chomsky 1981: 327 and (54b) is adapted from Safir 1985: 34; similar facts hold in Spanish, French, and German).

(54) a. *[PRO to be clear that we're out of fuel] would be a nuisance.
          (cf. *For it to be clear that we're out of fuel would be a nuisance*).
      b. *[PRO being obvious that John was late], the ceremony didn't start until 9 PM.
          (cf. *It being obvious that John was late, the ceremony didn't start until 9 PM*).

The emerging pragmatic picture of NOC is summarized in Landau (2021a) as follows.

(55) *Pragmatics of NOC*
      In a NOC configuration [... DP ... [PRO ...] ...] (order irrelevant), DP may control PRO iff:
      a. DP is [+topic] *or* a logophoric center.
      b. Default: [+topic] → [+human].

For further discussion of the competition between OC and NOC construals in adjuncts, see Landau (2021a: section 11.4).

5 A Dual Theory

In this section, I present a comprehensive attempt to unify complement control, NOC, and adjunct control, with special emphasis on the interaction of syntax and semantics in the realization of different control constructions (Landau 2015, 2018, 2020, 2021a,b). At the core of this theory is the idea that control clauses come in two types, which dictate two different modes of referential resolution: One type denotes a property, and the controller is identified by direct predication. The other type denotes a proposition whose subject is a "perspectival center," and the controller is identified by logophoric antecedence.

Dual theories of control are nothing new. Arguably, the very first theory in the field, by Rosenbaum (1967), was dual in nature, distinguishing between VP-complements, where the nonfinite VP is dominated by S only, and NP/PP-complements, where it is dominated by NP/PP over S. Later, Chomsky and Lasnik (1977) formulated a dual theory, where some control structures resulted from an OC rule (inserting PRO), and others result from a Reflexive Deletion rule, the intention being to distinguish OC structures that alternate with *for*-infinitives (and can be related to them by Reflexive Deletion) from those that do not.

Shortly after, Williams (1980) introduced his own OC-NOC distinction on the same empirical basis. Importantly, Williams was the first to propose (within the syntactic approaches to control) that OC should be reduced to predication, while NOC was analyzed as coindexation. This distinction was reincarnated in Lexical functional Grammar as the distinction between Functional Control and Anaphoric Control (Bresnan 1982, Mohanan 1983). Meanwhile, practitioners of Government and Binding hypothesized that PRO is anaphoric in IP complements and pronominal in CP complements (Bouchard 1984, Koster 1984). Within minimalism, Landau's (2001, 2004, 2008) Agree model of OC proposed two "routes": direct Agree between T/v and PRO or indirect Agree through the embedded C. Finally, restructuring-oriented studies have consistently assumed two mechanisms of associating the embedded external argument with a matrix controller: one involving an independent null subject (non-restructuring), and the other involving a reduced complement with no syntactic subject (restructuring); see Wurmbrand (2002, 2003) and Grano (2015).

Perhaps the most immediate precursors of the dual theory to be presented here are Wurmbrand (2002) and Williams (1992). Wurmbrand proposed that controlled complement clauses may be predicative or propositional, depending on the selecting predicate. Williams proposed that controlled adjuncts combine either by predication or by logophoric anchoring. Put together, the essence of the dual theory is that the controller of a predicative clause is the argument saturating the clause, whereas the controller of a propositional clause is the argument serving as antecedent to the logophoric element in the clause. This theory will now be applied to complement clauses (Section 5.1) and to adjunct clauses (Section 5.2).

5.1 The Two-Tiered Theory: Complement Control

The starting point of the Two-Tiered Theory of Control (henceforth, TTC) is the recognition that Williams' fundamental insight was correct: Some understood subjects are interpreted by predication while others require reference to some "logophoric" representation of antecedents. Let us consider OC by predication first.

That predication must be involved in some cases of OC is uncontroversial; reduced complements in restructuring environments, presumably, do not project a subject position, hence their external argument is shared with that of the matrix predicate via complex predicate formation (Wurmbrand 2002, 2003). What Landau (2015) proposed, adopting earlier analyses by Chomsky (1980), Chierchia (1990), and Clark (1990), is that clausal complements can also function as predicates if their PRO subject is treated as an operator. Specifically, a Fin head attracts PRO to its specifier, and the resulting chain is interpreted as λ-abstraction over the subject position. This is possible because PRO is a minimal pronoun devoid of any inherent denotation; hence, it cannot saturate a predicate, only form one. FinP is the projection where finiteness is encoded (Rizzi 1997); while propositional, full clauses project a CP layer above FinP (see (58)), predicative clauses lack that layer.

(56) *Predicative clause*: [$_{FinP}$ PRO$_i$ Fin [$_{TP}$ ~~PRO$_i$~~ ...]]

What type of predicates instantiate OC this way, namely, by taking a predicative complement? These are the same predicates that do not license PC (see Section 3.1). Their common semantic property is that they do not introduce attitudes.[24]

(57) *Predicative control: nonattitude predicates*
  a. Implicatives
      dare, manage, make sure, bother, remember, get, see fit, condescend, try, avoid, forget, fail, refrain, decline, neglect, force, compel.
  b. Aspectual
      begin, start, continue, finish, stop, resume.
  c. Modal
      have, need, may, should, is able, must.
  d. Evaluative (adjectives)
      rude, silly, smart, kind, (im)polite, bold, modest, cruel, cowardly, crazy.

From the semantic point of view, this is a heterogeneous class. All but the modal predicates carry some actuality entailment. Thus, positive implicative verbs (*remember*) and evaluative predicates (*rude*) entail their complement, while negative implicative verbs (*forget*) entail its negation. Aspectual verbs (*continue*) entail that the complement holds to some (possibly incomplete) degree. While some of the verbs select experiencers, the truth or falsity of the complement is evaluated not against the mental attitude of that experiencer but rather against the actual world; this is what defines these verbs as nonattitude. On Landau's (2015) analysis, a direct predication relation is established between the controller and the nonfinite complement. The resulting state of affairs is asserted to hold either in the actual world or (in the case of modal complements) in a set of possible worlds conforming to some norm. It is a defining feature of predicative control that the bearer of the property denoted by the complement is the referent of the controller *in the actual world*. Things are different in logophoric control, to which we now turn.

---

[24] Aspectual and modal verbs are often ambiguous between raising and control; we restrict attention to control variants in this discussion.

If predicative clauses constitute the first tier of OC, logophoric clauses are constructed as a second tier above them: A "perspectival" C head takes the FinP predicate of (56) as a complement, and projects a null *pro* as a specifier. This *pro* is associated (via a lexical presupposition on C) with a coordinate of the reported context – either the AUTHOR or ADDRESSEE of the matrix clause.[25] The OC dependency is broken into two links: variable binding between the controller and *pro*, and predication between *pro* and FinP. Because PRO mediates this predication relation (being the λ-operator that binds the embedded subject position), it shares the features that *pro* received from the controller, and the FinP property is understood as holding of the AUTHOR or ADDRESSEE of the matrix clause. Note that the OC complement (= CP) denotes a proposition, differently from the OC complement (= FinP) of predicative control verbs, which denotes a property. This fundamental distinction has important repercussions, as we will see in the following.

(58)   Logophoric clause: $[_{CP}\ pro\ C_{+log}\ [_{FinP}\ PRO_i\ Fin\ [_{TP}\ \text{PRO}_i\ \ldots]]]$

The predicates instantiating OC by taking a logophoric complement are the same predicates that license PC. Their common semantic property is that they *do* introduce attitudes.

(59)   *Logophoric control: attitude predicates*
   a. Factives
      glad, sad, regret, like, dislike, hate, loath, surprised, shocked, sorry.
   b. Propositional
      believe, think, suppose, imagine, say, claim, assert, affirm, declare, deny.
   c. Desideratives
      want, prefer, yearn, arrange, hope, afraid, refuse, agree, plan, aspire, offer, decide, mean, intend, resolve, strive, demand, promise, choose, eager, ready.
   d. Interrogatives
      wonder, ask, find out, interrogate, inquire, contemplate, deliberate, guess, grasp, understand, know, unclear.

In these OC complements, one observes the obligatory *de se* reading (when AUTHOR-controlled) or *de te* reading (when ADDRESSEE-controlled) of PRO; see Morgan (1970), Chierchia (1990), Percus and Sauerland (2003), Schlenker (2003), von Stechow (2003), Anand (2006), Pearson (2016, 2018), Hintzen and Martin (2021), and Pearson and Roeper (2022). These readings are consistently

---

[25] This idea is embedded in a well-established conception of the left periphery of clauses, which assumes that speech act participants are syntactically represented and active in a variety of grammatical processes (see, among others, Bianchi 2003, Safir 2004, Speas 2004, Hill 2007, Baker 2008, Sigurðsson 2011, Haegeman and Hill 2013, Wiltschko and Heim 2016, Sundaresan 2018, 2021, Zu 2018, Charnavel 2019, Deal 2020, Woods 2021, Baker and Ikawa 2024).

typical of OC under attitude predicates (but not of OC elsewhere). What they amount to is the observation that an attitude OC complement contributes information not about the matrix subject (AUTHOR) or object (ADDRESSEE), but rather about "the image" these participants have in the eyes of the attitude holder; technically, the "doxastic counterparts" of the matrix participants.

The specific character of *de se*/*de te* readings emerges in situation of misidentification, either of the self or of the addressee.

(60)   *Obligatory* de se
     Context: John watches a clip of himself, caught on CCTV camera, making suspicious moves near some house at night. He doesn't recognize himself but comes to believe that the person he watches is a burglar.
     a. John$_i$ hoped that he$_i$ would be caught.   *de re*: true
     b. John$_i$ hoped [PRO$_i$ to be caught].   *de se*: false

(61)   *Obligatory* de te
     Context: Betty is about to take Johnny to the movies. Earlier, Johnny messed up the living room, but Betty thinks it was Billy who did it. She tells Johnny: "Whoever messed up the living room should tidy it up!"
     a. Betty told Johnny$_i$ that [he$_i$ should tidy up the living room].   *de re*: true
     b. Betty told Johnny$_i$ [PRO$_i$ to tidy up the living room].   *de te*: false

Although *de se* readings in attitude OC contexts were thought to be unshakable, recent work suggests that at least with some OC verbs they are pragmatically defeasible. Pearson and Roeper (2022) observe that in contexts of ignorance disclaimers, such as *unwittingly*/*unintentionally*/*unknowingly*, or under the scope of *in effect*, the *de se* entailment is excluded. They describe a context in which Mary is the judge of a baking contest and, blindfolded, tastes her own cookie without recognizing it, and then declares that whoever baked that cookie deserves the prize. The following statements are all judged true in this scenario, despite the fact that Mary made (or intended) no first person statement of the kind "I deserve the prize."

(62) a. Mary$_i$ unwittingly/unintentionally/unknowingly claimed
        [PRO$_i$ to deserve the prize].
     b. Without realizing it/In effect, Mary$_i$ claimed [PRO$_i$ to deserve the prize].
     c. Mary didn't realize it, but she$_i$ claimed [PRO$_i$ to deserve the prize].

Taking *in effect* as their leading cue, Pearson and Roeper write:

> *In effect* does not suspend the requirement that PRO be *de se*, but rather it gives rise to apparent *de re* readings in contexts where it is irrelevant to some goal (e.g., giving a prize) whether the first person condition is met. In such contexts, an *in effect* PRO-sentence may be judged true even if the first person condition

is not met, if (i) the corresponding *de re* report happens to be true, and (ii) the outcomes of the proposition expressed by the *de re* report and the (counterfactual) outcomes of the proposition expressed by the PRO-sentences are in all relevant respects the same. (Pearson and Roeper 2022: 874)

Notably, Pearson and Roeper do not describe the readings in (62) as *de re*; these readings just share a certain property with *de re* (namely, foregrounding the speaker's perspective). It is thus still possible to maintain that *de se* is definitional for PRO in attitude OC. Furthermore, the "excluded entailment" effect is lexically restricted; while present with *claim*, it is unavailable with *want* (see Pearson and Roeper 2022 for details of the explanation).

Proceeding with the implications of *de se* construals, Landau (2018) pointed out there is a tension between the leading accounts of how PRO comes to be obligatorily construed *de se* (or *de te*) and the leading accounts of how it comes to agree with the controller. In the former category, we have semantic models that take OC complements to denote properties or centered worlds (Chierchia 1984, 1990, von Stechow 2003, Stephenson 2010, Pearson 2013). In these models, PRO is bound by a λ-operator located at the edge of the complement. This operator guarantees that the OC complement be of the right semantic type required by the attitude verb. Crucially, however, the operator bears no syntactic relation to the controller; they are only related in the semantics, and indirectly so. Thus, the robust fact of agreement in OC is left unexplained, assuming, as is standard, that agreement piggybacks *some* syntactic relation.

It is worth noting that the prospects of reducing agreement to semantic matching between the controller and PRO are rather grim. This can be seen with imposter or hybrid nouns, evincing a split between their formal and semantic features. The imposter noun *the present authors* governs either third person (formal) or first person (semantic) agreement (63a) (adapted from Collins and Postal 2012: 19), and the German hybrid noun *Mädchen* governs either neuter gender (formal) or feminine gender (semantic) agreement (63b) (Wurmbrand, pers. comm.). The features of PRO are detectable on embedded, agreeing reflexives and pronouns, which must be locally bound by PRO.

(63) a. The present authors$_i$ plan [PRO$_i$ to devote themselves/ourselves to ecology].
     b. Das Mädchen hat versprochen, [PRO$_i$ sein/ihr Bestes zu geben].
        the girl   has promised,   its/her best to give
        "The girl promised to do her best."

Without entering the intricate morphosyntax of hybrid nouns, suffice it to say that the mere availability of formal, nonsemantic agreement in attitude OC complements is an insurmountable obstacle for any attempt to reduce agreement to semantic matching. For semantic matching must make reference to the denotational values of the observed φ-features of PRO. However, these values can be either mismatched with the reference of the controller, or just uninterpretable. Thus, agreement in OC, including attitude OC, is an irreducible *syntactic* phenomenon. This phenomenon finds a natural explanation in the TTC insofar as it invokes variable binding and insofar as variable binding is a standard vehicle of agreement (Heim 2008, Kratzer 2009). By contrast, within the popular property-based view of OC, the explanation of agreement is "somewhat stipulative on every account" (Schlenker 2011: 1575).

Looking beyond agreement and *de se*, the TTC makes a range of predictions that have been largely confirmed. The first set of predictions follows from the highly strict nature of predication, which resists different types of "noncanonical" OC. Thus, control shift and split control are excluded with predicative complements but allowed (in principle) in logophoric ones. This is because a predicate in a given structure can only apply to a unique argument, whereas the intermediary logophoric *pro* in (58) can be anchored to either AUTHOR or ADDRESSEE coordinates, or possibly to their sum (Madigan 2008b). Likewise, "partial" readings are not obtainable under direct predication but can be modeled via an intermediate pronoun (see, e.g., Matsuda 2019). For this reason, PC is typical of attitude complements.[26]

The possibility of implicit control into predicative complements is less clear. Landau (2015) argued (following Landau 2010) that predicates must be saturated by overt arguments, and therefore controllers may not be implicit in aspectual or implicative constructions, as opposed to desiderative ones. In (64), this is illustrated with subject control verbs in Hebrew, where the controller becomes implicit upon passivization.

(64)　a.　*Logophoric control*
　　　　huxlat / tuxnan / huvtax　　　　　　　　　le'hitkadem ba-proyekt.
　　　　was.decided / was.planned / was.promised to.move.forward in.the.project
　　　　'It was decided/planned/promised to move forward with the project.'
　　　b.　*Predicative control*
　　　　*hufsak / nusa / niškax　　　　　　　le'hitkadem　　　ba-proyekt.
　　　　was.stopped / was.tried / was.forgotten to.move.forward in.the-project
　　　　'It was stopped/tried/forgotten to move forward with the project.'

The same split is attested with object control verbs in Hebrew: Object drop is possible only with desiderative verbs and not with implicative verbs.

---

[26] Experimental testing of PC largely confirms the correlation between attitude complements and tolerance to PC, yet finer-grained differences in the degree of tolerance have been found across various subtypes of attitude complements (White and Grano 2014).

(65) a. *Logophoric object control*

ha-menahel	civa / pakad / asar / laxac	(alay)
the-manager	ordered / commanded / prohibited / pressured	(on.me)
lešatef	pe'ula ba-misrad.	
to.cooperate	action in.the-office	

"The manager ordered / commanded / forbade / pressured (me)
to cooperate in the office."

    b. *Predicative object control*

Gil	kafa / hikša / hekel / hišpia	*(alay)
Gil	compelled/made.it.difficult/made.it.easy/influenced	*(on.me)
le'hitpater etmol.		
to.quit yesterday		

"Gil compelled / made it difficult for / made it easy for / influenced *(me) to
quit yesterday."

Against this evidence from Landau (2015) (who cites parallel data in Polish
and Russian), Pitteroff and Schäfer (2019) point out that examples parallel to
(64b), such as the Dutch example (66), are possible in a number of Germanic
languages, although there is "huge variation" in judgments.

(66)

Er	werd	vergeten/verzuimd	(om)	als	collectief	te	spelen,
there	was	forgotten/missed	C	as	collective	to	play,
juist	wat	normaliter	de	sterke	kracht	is	van het team.
just	what	normally	the	strong	power	is	of this team.

"People forgot/failed to play as a collective, which usually is the strength of this team."

It is notable that counterexamples to (65b) have not been reported.[27] One
can tentatively conclude that cross-linguistic variation in the control cap-
acity of implicit arguments is only attested with implicit *agents* of passive.
Recent work indeed suggests that the binary distinction between Active and
Passive Voice is an oversimplification; Voice heads come in different degrees
of "strength" and featural specification (Legate 2021, Sigurðsson and Wood
2021). It is thus quite possible that these Voice heads, or the external arguments they project, would correspondingly vary in their visibility to grammatical dependencies such as control, predication, and binding. Fleshing out
the details of such a typology is a task for future research.

Let us mention two further consequences of the TTC, one concerning the
size of the control complement and the other concerning its *semantic type*.
Comparing (56) and (58), we observe that predicative clauses are smaller than
logophoric ones, lacking at least the CP layer (and even more layers in
restructuring complements). This is to be expected insofar as the former

---

[27] It is assumed, of course, that implicit objects can be reliably distinguished from object *pro*; the
latter is expected to face no difficulties in controlling a predicative complement.

express modality, manipulation, phasal status, and achievement, while the latter express desires, fears, epistemic states, and speech acts. Typological research has shown that clausal complements of the latter type are larger than those of the former type, the difference keyed to the occurrence of designated heads in the left periphery of the clause, encoding the different types of attitudes (Lohninger and Wurmbrand 2024).

Concretely, to the extent that such functional heads are spelled out, we expect the left-periphery of logophoric complements to be more richly specified than that of predicative complements. Looking at complementizers, this tendency is consistent, although often concealed due to the common syncretism between functional heads in the left periphery (usually at most one is pronounced). In some languages, infinitival complementizers distribute across verb classes with hardly any systematic restrictions (i.e., *a/de/di* prepositional complementizers in Romance, *að* in Icelandic); in others, attitude complements are introduced by overt complementizers and nonattitude complements are not. Notably, no language exhibits the opposite pattern (overt complementizers in nonattitude complements and no complementizer in attitude complements).

As an illustration, consider the distribution of the Polish complementizer *żeby* (Bondaruk 2004, Citko 2012). It is obviative with subjunctive complements and with some desiderative infinitival complements. With object control verbs and a few subject control verbs, it has no effect on control, but with many subject control verbs its presence licenses NC. What is relatively clear is that predicative complements (modal, aspectual, and implicative) reject *żeby*; it only occurs in logophoric complements. For example, *żeby* may or must occur with desiderative and epistemic subject control complements (67b) and (67c) but not with implicative complements (67a).

(67) a. Jan$_i$　zdołał　[(*żeby) PRO$_{i/*j}$ śpiewać].
　　　　Jan　managed　C　　　　　　sing.INF
　　　　"Jan managed to sing."

　　b. Jan$_i$　wolał　[PRO$_{i/*j}$ śpiewać] / Jan$_i$ wolał　[żeby *pro*$_{*i/j}$ śpiewać].
　　　　Jan　preferred　　sing.INF Jan preferred C　　　sing.INF
　　　　"Jan preferred to sing. / Jan preferred for others to sing."

　　c. Jan marzył　[*(żeby) PRO$_{i/*j}$ śpiewać].
　　　　Jan dreamed　C　　　　　sing.INF
　　　　"Jan dreamed to sing."

A parallel contrast exists between implicative and desiderative object control complements.

(68) a. Marek$_i$ dał mi [(*żeby) PRO$_{i/*j}$ poprowadzić swój samochód].
   Mark let me C drive.INF his car
   "Mark let me drive his car."

   b. Jan kazał Piotrowi$_i$ [(żeby) PRO$_{i/*j}$ nie biegać po ulicy].
   John told Peter C not run.INF on street
   "John told Peter not to run on the street."

A similar distribution is displayed by the jussive modals *yao* "must/will/ want" and its negative counterpart *bie* "NEG.IMP" and *bu-yao* "NEG-should /NEG.IMP" in Mandarin Chinese (Liao and Wang 2022). These are banned from predicative OC complements (69) (which must use standard negation instead) and occur only in logophoric ones (70) (note that (70b) exhibits PC as well). Liao and Wang analyze them semantically as the imperative operator of Stegovec (2019) and identify them with Landau's C^{OC}, the complementizer of logophoric OC complements.

(69) a. Zhangsan$_i$ kaishi [**bie/bu** PRO$_i$ zai-nali tiaowu].
   Zhangsan start NEG.IMP/NEG in-there dance
   "Zhangsan started to not dance in that place."

   b. Zhangsan$_i$ neng(gou) [**bie/bu** PRO$_i$ zheme zuo].
   Zhangsan can NEG.IMP/NEG so do
   "Zhangsan is able to not do so."

(70) a. Zhangsan$_i$ dasuan [**bie/*bu** PRO$_i$ tai-zao jiehun].
   Zhangsan intend NEG.IMP/NEG too-early marry
   "Zhangsan intended not to get married too young."

   b. Zhangsan quan Lisi$_i$ [**bie/*bu** PRO$_{i+}$ zai-liu-dian jianmian].
   Zhangsan persuade Lisi NEG.IMP/NEG at-six-o'clock meet
   "Zhangsan persuaded Lisi not to meet at six."

In fact, it is not required that the Fin head of predicative complements be null, as long as it is distinct from the C head of logophoric complements. A language where both heads are overt and distinct may well be Moro (Kordofanian; South Sudan), as documented in Jenks and Rose (2017). The complementizer *nə̀-* only occurs in implicative complements (71a), whereas the complementizer *t̪á* only occurs in logophoric complements (71b).[28]

(71) a. kúk:u g-əndət̪ʃən-ú (**n**)-áŋɔ̀ -$^↓$lə́vət̪ʃ-a ŋál:o(-ŋ)
   Kuku CLg-(RTC-)try-PFV C-3SG.INF-hide-INF Ngalo-ACC
   "Kuku tried to hide Nghalo."

---

[28] Jenks and Rose (2017) observe that the attitude verb *-bwáŋ-* "want" also takes a *nə̀*-infinitive; this may be a case of restructuring, which is common with this verb cross-linguistically. They also note that *-ámad̪at̪-* "help" alternates between the two complement types, which likely reflects different interpretations (implicative or not). The dataset from Moro is quite limited and further study is no doubt needed to fully understand the distribution of the two complementizers.

b. é-g-a-mwandəð-ó   kúk:u-ŋ   **ṭá** ɜ́ŋ-ɔ́-↓búg-í   ís:íə.
    1SG-CLg-RTC-ask-PFV Kuku-ACC C   3SG.INF-give-INF   CLj.gun
    "I asked Kuku to shoot the gun."

What is even more striking is that *nə̂-* also introduces nonsubject relative clauses in Moro. Given the predicative analysis of OC in (71a), it is a pleasant convergence to find the same complementizer introducing both predicative OC complements and predicative modifier clauses.

A final cross-linguistic pattern that naturally falls into place under the TTC involves the tolerance of OC complements to lexical subjects. While attitude and nonattitude complements exhibit the same OC signature when their subject is null (except for the *de se*/*de te* property), they differ dramatically in their tolerance to a lexical subject: Only attitude complements allow it.

(72) Complements of attitude predicates allow lexical subjects; complements of non-attitude predicates *dis*allow lexical subjects.

Generaization (72) is very broad. It crucially abstracts away from the syntactic realization of the complement – finite or not, nominalized or not, and so on. It was first stated by Grano (2015: 19) in terms of the EC-PC contrast, but we have seen that this contrast reflects the deeper cut between attitude and nonattitude complements.

In some languages, no special grammatical device is needed to license a lexical subject in an infinitival complement (thus turning it from OC to NC); this is the situation in Malayalam (Mohanan 1982) and in Tamil (Sundaresan and McFadden 2009), the latter illustrated in (73). Note that a null subject is obligatorily controlled under both the implicative *try* and the desiderative *want*, but a lexical subject is tolerated only under *want*.

(73) a. raman$_i$ [PRO$_{i/*j}$/(*Anand) saadatt-ai saappiḍ-a]   paa-tt-aan.
          Raman.NOM   Anand rice-ACC   eat.INF   try-PST−3 M.SG
          "Raman tried (*Anand) to eat rice."
      b. champa-vukku$_i$ [PRO$_{i/*j}$/Sudha oru samosa-vai saappiḍ-a] veṇḍ-um.
          Champa-DAT   Sudha a samosa-ACC eat-INF   want−3 N.SG
          "Champa wants (Sudha) to eat a samosa."

The contrast appears to be replicated in English, but this is only because *want* is an ECM verb, which can license an embedded subject, as opposed to, for example, *decide*. What is quite clear in the Dravidian languages in that the embedded subject is licensed regardless of the *particular* matrix verb; all attitude complements, finite or nonfinite, accept lexical subjects. Even more striking evidence comes from Irish, a language notorious for its free licensing of (accusative) lexical subjects in infinitives (McCloskey 1980a, 1985, McCloskey and Sells 1988, Bondaruk 2006). Yet McCloskey (1980b) observed that the nonfinite complements of *some* predicates reject a lexical subject. Although he has not attempted any generalization, the examples he provided, given in (74a) and (74b), contain modal and implicative verbs, namely, nonattitude predicates (Irish infinitives are formed from Verbal Nouns [VN], usually following the particle *a*). Attitude predicates, on the other hand, allow either OC or NC ((74c) and (74d) are from Bondaruk 2006, and (74e) is from McCloskey 1985).

(74) *Nonattitude infinitival complements in Irish:* ✓*PRO,* *lexical subject

    a. Ní thiocfadh *pro*ᵢ libh [PROᵢ/*Nollaig imeacht   chomh luath sin.
       NEG could.2SG   Noel   leave.VN   so.early
       "You couldn't (*Noel) leave so early."

    b. Rinne   séᵢ   iarracht [PROᵢ/*na   daoine teach   a   thógáil].
       made   he   attempt   those   people house   PRT   build.VN
       "He tries (*those people) to build houses."

    Attitude infinitival complements in Irish: ✓*PRO,* ✓*lexical subject*

    c. Ba   mhaith   liom *pro*ᵢ [PROᵢ imeacht / é   a   meacht].
       COP   good   with.1SG   go.VN   him   PRT   go.VN
       "I would like (him) to go."

    d. Tá   mé   sásta [PROᵢ   a   bheith   anseo].
       am   I   glad   PRT   be.VN   here
       "I'm glad to be here."

    e. Bheinn   sásta   [iad   a   bheith   i láthair].
       I.would.be glad   them   PRT   be.VN   present
       "I would be glad for them to be present."

To see the effect of (72) in English, observe that *for*-infinitivals are excluded in nonattitude complements (Grano 2015: 19). The marginal acceptability of lexical subjects in the complements of certain implicative verbs, as in (75b), is due to lexical coercion, by which the core meaning of the verb is modified or extended (see Jackendoff and Culicover 2003, Grano 2017b). However, language-internal factors, partly arbitrary in nature, somewhat obscure the picture of English infinitivals. For example, not all desiderative verbs take a *for*-infinitive (75c), and *wh*-infinitivals, although expressing attitudes, consistently reject lexical subjects (75d) (Chomsky and Lasnik 1977).

(75)   a.   * John began/had [for Bill to solve the problem].
        b.   # John tried/managed [for Bill to solve the problem].
        c.   * Mary persuaded Fred [for the kids to buy ice cream].
        d.   * She wondered [where (* (for) people) to go].

All these "irregularities" of infinitives disappear under finite complementation, where lexical subjects are uniformly licensed. The problem is that nonattitude predicates also reject finite complements, so there does not seem to be any clean testing ground in English where the empirical consequences of (72) can be fully observed across the attitude–nonattitude divide.

In fact, there is one testing ground that overcomes these difficulties – gerunds. English gerunds have no trouble licensing an internal subject. Therefore, when placed in complement position, the (non)availability of a lexical subject inside the gerund purely reflects general principles. As it happens, it precisely reflects (72).

Pires (2007) pointed out that gerundive complements fall into two classes: One class, which he described as [+tense], accepts either PRO or a lexical subject, whereas the other class, [–tense], only accepts a PRO subject. Following Landau's (2015) restatement of the [±tense] distinction in terms of [±attitude], this split is aligned with (72).

(76) *Nonattitude gerundive complements:* ✓*PRO, *lexical subject*
　　a. Philip$_i$ tried/avoided [PRO$_i$/*Jane driving in the freeway].
　　b. Jane$_i$ started/resumed [PRO$_i$/*Frank talking to us].

　　Attitude gerundive complements: ✓*PRO,* ✓*lexical subject*
　　c. Sue$_i$ favored/insisted on [PRO$_i$/Anna moving to Chicago].
　　d. They$_i$ imagined/suggested [PRO$_i$/Paul joining the trip].

English has another variant of gerundive complementation, where the gerund is introduced by a preposition. These P-gerund constructions, studied in Landau (2021b), also fall into two broad categories: a causative-implicative class and a nonimplicative class. Each class consists of several subclasses, depending on the preposition involved. What is crucial to note is that all and only the complements of the implicative (nonattitude) verbs reject a lexical subject.

(77) *Nonattitude P-gerund complements:* ✓*PRO, *lexical subject*
　　a. She fooled us$_i$ into [PRO$_i$/*Bob) thinking she was sick].
　　b. They confined Beth$_i$ to [PRO$_i$/*her son's eating dog food].
　　c. John talked Sue's partner$_i$ out of [PRO$_i$/*her accepting a bribe].
　　d. John restrained Sue$_i$ from [PRO$_i$/*her candidate's making
　　　　a long statement].

　　Attitude P-gerund complements: ✓*PRO,* ✓*lexical subject*
　　e. He$_i$ accused me of [PRO$_i$/Frank being suspended].
　　f. Bill credits Jane$_i$ with [PRO$_i$/David finding the courage to resist].
　　g. I'd caution you$_i$ against [PRO$_i$/anyone taking this too far for now].

As Landau (2021b) shows, this split is correlated with a cluster of other contrasts, all predictable from the different ways in which control is established in predicative constructions as opposed to logophoric constructions.

Generalization (72) falls out naturally from the TTC's commitment to the underlying duality of OC complementation – (56) versus (58). In predicative control, the complement denotes a predicate; specifically, the derived predicate FinP. In logophoric control, the complement denotes a proposition; specifically, the proposition obtained from applying the predicative FinP to the logophoric *pro* in [Spec,CP]. Thus, control complements do come in two semantic types, contra the uniformist property-theories stemming from Chierchia 1984, but in line with the fundamental duality envisioned in Wurmbrand (2002). Because nonattitude verbs select properties, their complements cannot host a lexical subject, which would saturate the property and yield a type mismatch. Because attitude verbs select propositions, their complements may surface with a lexical subject. Importantly, *either* (58) (with PRO) *or* a clause with a lexical subject may satisfy the selectional requirement for a proposition. While the latter option is not consistently available in all nonfinite environments (due to poorly under-stood distributional restrictions), it is robust enough in those environments that allow a "fair" testing.

In the next section, we will see how the property–proposition divide extends further to account for the fundamental arrangement of nonfinite adjuncts with respect to control.

5.2 The Two-Tiered Theory: Adjunct Control

Throughout much of the history of work on control, adjuncts have received considerably less attention than complements. Some major theories of control have been developed without considering adjuncts at all (Sag and Pollard 1991, Landau 2000, Jackendoff and Culicover 2003); others mention adjuncts sum-marily, illustrating one or two types at the most, only to assimilate them to standard OC (Manzini 1983, Mohanan 1983, Clark 1990, Hornstein 1999, 2003, Pires 2007, Fischer 2018, McFadden and Sundaresan 2018). This situation has fortunately changed in recent years, with concentrated studies of adjunct control that pay much closer attention to the different types of adjuncts, their modifica-tional flavor and how it relates to the OC/NOC classification (Green 2018, 2019, Landau 2021a, Fischer and Flaate Høyem 2022; see Williams 1992 for an important precursor). In this section, I lay out the major results of this recent work and the research questions it raises.

It was Williams (1992) who first pointed out that adjuncts display a dual behavior: Sometimes they pattern with OC and sometimes with NOC. Following earlier observations in Chomsky (1981: 324–327), Williams noted that PRO in NOC must be [+human], a feature he attributed to its logophoric nature. Obligatory control, in contrast, operates by predication, accepting inanimate subjects and even weather-*it*. By way of illustration, consider the following examples.

(78)   a.   Around here, it can't snow [before PRO$_i$ raining].   *OC*
       b.   There won't be any progress [without PRO insisting   *NOC*
            on guidance from the outside].

Williams assumed that OC and NOC adjuncts are attached at different heights; specifically, that NOC adjuncts are higher than the subject. This idea is part of what Landau (2021b: 93) calls "the classical view." On this view, OC and NOC in adjuncts are in complementary distribution, because (i) OC requires c-command by the controller, NOC does not, and (ii) OC is mandatory whenever possible (NOC is "last resort"). It follows from the classical view that NOC adjuncts are not c-commanded by the subject.[29]

However, Green (2018) and Landau (2021b) marshal a series of arguments refuting the classical view. To begin with, OC and NOC are not mutually exclusive. Although normally in competition, the nature of this competition is pragmatic rather than grammatical, hence it is not a rigid constraint. Careful testing reveals that OC and NOC can even coexist in the same sentence (Green 2018: 40). Thus, "last resort" and "elsewhere case" are the wrong concepts to describe the interplay between OC and NOC in adjuncts.

(79)   The pool$_i$ was the perfect temperature [after PRO$_{i/arb}$ being in the hot sun all day].

Second, NOC adjuncts can demonstrably attach below the subject. As Landau (2021b: 95–96) shows, they can scope below negation and be elided as part of VP-ellipsis. Note that the rationale clause in (80a) involves speaker-control and the temporal clause in (80b) involves arbitrary control, two types of NOC.

(80)   a.   The door is not open in order to greet anyone, I just needed some fresh air.
       b.   In the summer, the night sky is frequently an unforgettable spectacle
            when camping in the desert, but in the winter it rarely is.

Third, even lower adjuncts, located inside the VP, may display NOC. Consider Object Purpose Clauses, whose embedded object is bound by (an operator bound by) the matrix theme, and whose PRO subject may display NOC. The following examples demonstrate that this NOC reading persists even though the adjunct is necessarily VP-internal (hence, resists stranding under VP-ellipsis).

---

[29] For proponents of the classical view, see Williams (1980), Lebeaux (1984), Jones (1992), Kawasaki (1993), Hornstein (1999, 2003), Landau (2000, 2013: 254), Manzini and Roussou (2000), Boeckx and Hornstein (2007), Boeckx et al. (2010), Fischer (2018), McFadden and Sundaresan (2018), Fischer and Flaate Høyem (2022).

(81) a. The sterile bandages have been placed in the small backpack
[PRO$_{arb}$ to use in case of serious injury],
and the plasters have been ___ too.

b. * The sterile bandages have been placed in the small backpack
[PRO$_{arb}$ to use in case of serious injury],
but the plasters have been ___ [PRO$_{arb}$ to use for bruises only].

Conversely, TP-adjuncts may display OC despite claims that this position is reserved for NOC (e.g., Fischer and Flaate Høyem 2022). In (82), the matrix subject can be neither a logophoric antecedent (being inanimate) nor a topic (being a negative quantifier). Correspondingly, it does not qualify for NOC. The observed control relation into the initial adjunct, therefore, must be OC.

(82) After falling into this acid, nothing survives.

See Landau (2021b: 94–98) for further, extensive evidence against the classical view.[30]

Instead of positing unmotivated correlations between an adjunct's position and the OC–NOC distinction, we should look for a theory that ties the structural position of adjuncts to something else. Landau (2021a) argues that this "something else" is *compositionality*: OC adjuncts and NOC adjuncts are of different semantic types, and this difference explains which syntactic nodes they may combine with (to yield an interpretable adjunction structure) versus which they cannot (due to a type mismatch). Crucially, the semantic-type distinction is the same fundamental distinction already assumed in the TTC for complement OC; namely, the distinction between predicative clauses and propositional clauses.

While complement clauses split into these two types directly, as in (56)/(58), adjunct clauses split indirectly, via a mediating P head. This P head may be overt (*before*, *without*, *in order*, etc.) or null, as it is in rationale clauses without *in order*, stimulus clauses (e.g., *He smiled to see my response*), and so on.

(83) a. Predicative adjunct: [$_{PP}$ P$_{Pred}$ [$_{FinP}$ PRO$_i$ Fin [$_{TP}$ ~~PRO$_i$~~ ...]]]
b. Propositional adjunct: [$_{PP}$ P$_{Prop}$ [$_{CP}$ *pro* C$_{+log}$ [$_{FinP}$ PRO$_i$ Fin [$_{TP}$ ~~PRO$_i$~~ ...]]]]

---

[30] As noted earlier, much existing work underestimates the availability of NOC with vP-adjuncts, due to confounded test examples, where the local subject is human and hence favored over any other antecedent *both* by the OC derivation and by the NOC derivation. Indeed, Fischer and Flaate Høyem (2022) present many examples, which are similarly confounded, to make this point for English, German, and Norwegian. They do provide a few examples with inanimate subjects where NOC is allegedly impossible (e.g., their (17) and (19)); but this does not seem to be true in general, as the following data from Landau (2021b: 109–110) indicate.

(i) Fortschritt wird hier nie   passieren, [ohne PRO$_{arb}$ eigene Fehler   zuzugeben]. *German*
progress will here never happen   without   own   mistakes to.admit.
"Progress will never happen here without admitting one's own mistakes."

(ii) Skjemaet må være ferdig utfyllt   [for PRO   å kunne gi   råd].   *Norwegian*
the.form must be finished filled.out for   to could give advice
"The form must be filled out completely in order to give advice."

The way these two semantic types map to control types is asymmetric. Propositional adjuncts can be realized either as NC (with a lexical subject inside the adjunct) or NOC. Predicative adjuncts can be realized either as strict OC adjuncts, namely, adjuncts that never alternate with NOC or NC, or as the OC variant of alternating OC/NOC adjuncts.

The understanding that controlled adjuncts split in this asymmetric fashion is fairly recent. Most earlier work simply assumed that adjuncts display OC or NOC. However, Green (2018, 2019) and Landau (2021a) established a sharp dichotomy between adjuncts that never alternate with NOC and those that do.

(84)   *Controlled adjuncts in English*
    a.   Strict OC adjuncts: Goal, Result, Stimulus, Subject Purpose Clause (SPC)
    b.   Alternating OC/NOC adjuncts: Object Purpose Clause (OPC), Rationale, Temporal, Absolutive, Justification, Telic.

For a full, systematic empirical description of all these adjuncts, see Landau (2021a). Here, we will just present a few illustrative contrasts. A result clause modifies an inchoative event by elaborating on its result (85a). As a strict OC adjunct, its controller must be the matrix subject and no other contextually available antecedent (85b), although this would be possible with a temporal adjunct (85c) on its NOC variant, as often happens when the local subject is inanimate.

(85)   a.   The door$_i$ opened again [PRO$_i$ to reveal a strangely decorated room].
    b.   *The door$_i$ opened again [PRO to try to close it$_i$].
    c.   The door$_i$ opened again [after PRO trying to close it$_i$]. (Green 2019: 16)

Because strict OC adjuncts are necessarily predicative, they require the presence of an overt controller (see (64b)/(65b)). Alternating OC/NOC adjuncts, on the other hand, may access an implicit controller via the propositional NOC route. We thus predict a contrast in tolerance to implicit control. The following examples compare an SPC (strict OC) and an OPC (alternating OC/NOC), confirming the prediction: Only the latter allows the controller to be dropped in the presence of the adjunct (note that the relevant objects *are* optional, in principle).

(86)   a.   We're now hiring (people).
    b.   We're now hiring *(people$_i$) [PRO$_i$ to manage the marketing for us].   *SPC*
    c.   They provided (me$_i$) a connector cable [PRO$_i$ to charge my   *OPC*
       device with].

The cut between the two kinds of adjuncts ultimately reflects the distinction between the basic semantic types – property versus proposition. One of

Landau's (2021a) main point is that this semantic type is independently detectable by the existence of a "propositional variant" for the controlled adjunct. A propositional variant for a controlled adjunct is an adjunct introduced by the same preposition, contributing the same modificational relation, except that it hosts a lexical subject. While some adjuncts allow an alternation between PRO and DP (... *without Bill/PRO saying much*), others restrict the propositional variant to finite clauses (... *while PRO watching TV / while Bill watched TV*). However, insofar as such a variant exists, it indicates that the adjunct head may either be P_{Pred} or P_{Prop}, and the adjunct is classified as alternating OC/NOC. When no such variant exists, the head of the adjunct is uniquely P_{Pred}, and the adjunct is classified as strict OC. The *propositional variant criterion* states that adjuncts without a propositional variant are strictly predicative and require strict OC, while adjuncts with a propositional variant are either predicative (OC) or propositional (NOC).

For example, a stimulus clause may not host a lexical subject but a Justification Clause may, (87a) versus (88a). Correspondingly, the former rejects non-c-commanding control (a sign of NOC), whereas the latter accepts it, (87b) versus (88b).

(87)   a.   Bill wept [(*for his wife) to hear the tragic story].
        b.   [Her$_i$ kids]$_j$ wept [PRO$_{j/*i}$ to hear the tragic story].

(88)   a.   Our life was blessed [for her being so much a part of it].
        b.   Her$_i$ kids were punished [for PRO$_i$ letting them ruin the place].

This state of affairs is summarized in table (89).

(89)   *S-selection in nonfinite adjuncts*

	Adjunct's head s-selects	**Propositional variant**
Strict OC adjuncts	Property	−
OC/NOC adjuncts	Property/proposition	+

It is striking that Strict NOC adjuncts are unattested. The best candidate for such adjuncts are speech act oriented (SAO) adjuncts (Quirk et al. 1985: 1068–1073, Kortmann 1991, Meinunger 2006, Lyngfelt 2009, Duffley 2014: 99–102), where PRO is controlled by the speaker in declarative contexts and by the addressee in interrogative contexts.

(90)   a.   [PRO judging from my/*your experience], John would be better off without Mary.
        b.   [PRO judging from your/*my experience], would John be better off without Mary?

However, Landau (2021a) points out that SAO adjuncts are subject to severe restrictions that do not generally apply to NOC adjuncts. First, while both types of adjuncts undergo perspectival shift when embedded, an SAO adjunct is uniquely anchored to either AUTHOR or ADDRESSEE, not both.

(91) a. *NOC adjunct* (PRO = reported AUTHOR/ADDRESSEE)
          John$_i$ told Mary$_j$ that [PRO$_{i/j}$ having such experience],
          this job would be a piece of cake.
      b. *SAO adjunct* (PRO = reported AUTHOR)
          John$_i$ told Mary$_j$ that [PRO$_{i/*j}$ judging from experience],
          such offers were very rare.

Tellingly, SAO adjuncts reject lexical subjects, unlike all other NOC adjuncts.

(92) a. *NOC adjunct*
          [His income now being secure], John is better off without Mary.
      b. *SAO adjunct*
          * [For me to be absolutely frank], John would be better off without Mary.

Landau proposes that SAO adjuncts are in fact OC adjuncts, predicated of a null nominal in the left periphery of the clause, representing the AUTHOR or ADDRESSEE.

Given this picture, table (89) represents a genuine asymmetry that calls for explanation. By default, *all* controlled adjuncts map to predicates; a subset of them maps to propositions, as an additional option. What is the source of the predicative default? Landau claims that it is rooted in *Economy of Projection* (EoP): All else being equal, a more minimal structure is favored over a less minimal one (Chomsky 1991, Safir 1993, Grimshaw 1994, Bošković 1996, Speas 2006). Looking at the structures of the two types of adjuncts in (83a) and (83b), it is clear that the predicative adjunct is more minimal than the propositional one, FinP being properly contained in CP. Predicative adjuncts account for all instances of local control; hence, they are the first choice of the child in parsing input conveying this interpretation. As positive evidence for a propositional variant, in the shape of adjuncts with lexical subjects, is gradually accumulated, the child would entertain an additional, propositional variant, along with the suitable head (P$_{Prop}$) (see Landau 2021a: 165–171 for developmental evidence). This, in turn, would grant these adjuncts the option of NOC.

Note that EoP only regulates the choice between different derivations of *the same interpretation*. Yet OC and NOC often compete for distinct interpretations. An oft-made observation is that a local human controller is strongly favored over any alternative construal, for example, long-distance or arbitrary control (Kortmann 1991, Kawasaki 1993, Lyngfelt 2000). This has led many researchers to misclassify adjunct control as OC, as in the Italian example (93a) (Sundaresan 2014). Yet if the matrix subject is inanimate, the same type of adjunct, in the same position, supports extra-sentential control (93b) (Landau 2021b: 106).

(93) a. [PRO$_{i/*j}$ detestando il pesce], Gianni$_i$ compró solo carne.
                 detest.GER the fish   Gianni bought only meat
        "[PRO$_{i/*j}$ detesting the fish], Gianni$_i$ bought only meat."
    b. [PRO detestando gli altri], la vita diventa difficile.
               hate.GER the others the life gets   difficult
        "Life gets difficult when one hates the others."

This preference is strong but not absolute (attesting to its pragmatic source). Occasionally, a local human controller can be skipped, as in the following examples from Español-Echevarría (2000: 101) and Green (2018: 36).

(94) a. Bill$_i$ will introduce the ambassador to the president [in order PRO to give him$_i$ the opportunity to observe their reactions].
    b. Strangely, the candidates talked avidly when we$_i$ asked them where they were from, but they hesitated [after PRO$_i$ asking them about their work].

Why is a local human controller so strongly favored, though? The answer is straightforward. The OC derivation is guided by the locality of predication, so it clearly picks out the local subject. The NOC derivation is guided by salience along two dimensions – logophoricity and topicality (see Section 4). A human antecedent is already ranked high on these two scales, as humans are the canonical perspective holders and also make better sentence topics (on the animacy hierarchy, see Comrie 1981, DuBois 1987, Song 2001, Swierskia 2004, Kuno 2006). Thus, in the common scenario of a local human subject, both the OC derivation and the NOC derivation converge on the same reading. Indeed, we might suppose that EoP will favor the OC derivation under these circumstances. Any nonlocal control interpretation would have to be supported by exceptional salience of the remote antecedent, surpassing that of the local human subject.

This indeed is quite rare, leading to the false impression that the OC reading somehow "blocks" the NOC reading. Strictly speaking, however, this never happens. Only when the readings coincide do the two derivations compete directly (and EoP adjudicates in favor of OC). Otherwise, the choice between the reading delivered by OC and the one (or several ones) delivered by NOC is a matter of degree, a complex interaction of pragmatic salience, processing, linear order, and so on. All too often the NOC reading will be ranked so low as to be practically inaccessible. Yet as far as the grammar is concerned, it is generated alongside the OC reading.

6 Open Questions and Challenges for Future Research

The goal of this Element has been to present the major approaches to the study of control within generative grammar, with an emphasis on the significant advances made during the last ten to fifteen years (up to 2023). In the first part of this Element, we have seen how the theoretical construct "obligatory control" has been gradually developed and refined in continual opposition to Raising and to pronominal anaphora. Both lexicalist and syntactic approaches contributed a wealth of observations and deepened our understanding of how control interacts with argument structure, event decomposition, and attitude ascription on the one hand, and binding, agreement, and case assignment on the other hand. Nonetheless, the limitations of these approaches have pushed many authors to pursue an alternative conception of OC, which assimilates it to the grammar of ESAs. Within this conception, parallels and differences are studied between OC and logophoric binding, indexical shift, and similar phenomena that lie at the syntax–pragmatics interface. While many questions remain open, this approach currently holds the most promise for the future study of OC, at least its manifestation in attitude complements.

In these concluding remarks, let me list the main challenges we still face in the study of control, in the hope that future research will focus its attention on their resolution.

(95)   *Current challenges to the study of control*
   a. **Backward/copy control**: What is the precise empirical scope of this phenomenon? What accounts for its rarity? How is it to be reconciled with ample evidence against a unified analysis of Raising and OC?
   b. **Partial control**: What is the best analysis of PC? Is it registered in the syntax or only in the semantics? Why does PC PRO resist distributivity?
   c. **Agreement**: Granted that PRO formally agrees with the controller, how is this to be captured under the property-based theory of OC or under the indexical-shift theory? How can these theories be modified so as to preserve their insights and yet accommodate agreement in a natural way?
   d. **The OC–NC generalization**: Why does agreement block OC in attitude complements, and why does this restriction (apparently) apply in some languages but not in others?
   e. **Overt PRO**: What demands the nullness of PRO in the general case and why is this demand lifted in certain languages? Why does the overtness of PRO depend on focus (or pitch accent) in some languages but not in others?
   f. **Adjunct control**: How does the modificational semantics of an adjunct determine its control status – strict OC or alternating OC/NOC? What loci of cross-linguistic variation are expected or attested in the susceptibility of adjuncts to control?

No doubt, substantive answers to these questions will not only advance our understanding of control but also generate novel puzzles and challenges in their turn. This, however, is only for the better.

References

Adesola, Oluseye. 2005. *Pronouns and Null Operators: Ā-dependencies and Relations in Yoruba*. PhD dissertation, Rutgers University.

Adler, Allison N. 2006. *Syntax and Discourse in the Acquisition of Adjunct Control*. PhD dissertation, MIT.

Alboiu, Gabriela. 2007. Moving Forward with Romanian Backward Control and Raising. In *New Horizons in the Analysis of Control and Raising*, ed. William D. Davies and Stanley Dubinsky, 187–211. Dordrecht: Springer.

Alexiadou, Artemis, and Anagnostopoulou, Elena. 2021. Backward Control, Long Distance Agree, Nominative Case and TP/CP Transparency. In *Non-canonical Control in a Cross-Linguistic Perspective*, ed. Anne Mucha, Jutta M. Hartmann, and Beata Trawiński, 15–34. Amsterdam: John Benjamins.

Allotey, Deborah. 2021. Overt Pronouns of Infinitival Predicates of Gã. *Western Papers in Linguistics* 4:1–47.

Anagnostopoulou, Elena, and Alexiadou, Artemis. 1999. Raising without Infinitives and the Nature of Agreement. In *Proceedings of WCCFL 18*, ed. Sonya Bird, Andrew Carnie, Jason D. Haugen, and Peter Norquest, 15–25. Somerville, MA: Cascadilla Press.

Anand, Pranav. 2006. *De De se*. PhD dissertation, MIT.

Anand, Pranav, and Nevins, Andrew. 2004. Shifty Operators in Changing Contexts. In *Proceedings of SALT 16*, ed. Robert B. Young, 20–37. Ithaca, NY: Cornell University.

Ariel, Mira. 1990. *Accessing Noun-Phrase Antecedents*. London: Routledge.

Authier, J.-Marc, and Reed, Lisa. 2018. Symmetric Reciprocal Semantics as a Predictor of Partial Control. *Linguistic Inquiry* 49:379–393.

Authier, J.-Marc, and Reed, Lisa A. 2020. Agreement and Pronouns: Implications for Partial Control. In *Romance Languages and Linguistic Theory 16*, ed. Irene Vogel, 19–36. Amsterdam: John Benjamins.

Bach, Emmon. 1979. Control in Montague Grammar. *Linguistic Inquiry* 10:515–531.

Baker, Mark. 2008. *The Syntax of Agreement and Concord*. Cambridge: Cambridge University Press.

Baker, Mark, and Ikawa, Shiori. 2024. Control Theory and the Relationship between Logophoric Pronouns and Logophoric Uses of Anaphors. *Natural Language and Linguistic Theory*. https://doi.org/10.1007/s11049-023-09592-3.

Baltin, Mark. 2009. The Properties of Negative Non-finite Complements. In *NYU Working Papers in Linguistics, Vol. 2: Papers in Syntax*, ed. Patricia Irwin and Violeta Vasquéz Rojas Maldonado, 1–17. New York: New York University.

Barbosa, Pilar. 2009. A Case for an Agree-Based Theory of Control. In *Proceedings of the 11th Seoul International Conference on Generative Grammar*, 101–123.

Baykov, Fyodor, and Rudnev, Pavel. 2020. Not All Obligatory Control Is Movement. *Journal of Linguistics* 56:893–906.

Bianchi, Valentina. 2003. On Finiteness as Logophoric Anchoring. In *Temps et Point de Vue / Tense and Point of View*, ed. Jacqueline Guéron and Liliane Tasmowski, 213–246. Nanterre: Université Paris X.

Bobaljik, Jonathan. 2008. Missing Persons: A Case Study in Morphological Universals. *The Linguistic Review* 25:203–230.

Bobaljik, Jonathan, and Landau, Idan. 2009. Icelandic Control Is Not A-movement: The Case from Case. *Linguistic Inquiry* 40:113–132.

Boeckx, Cedric, and Hornstein, Norbert. 2003. Reply to "Control Is Not Movement." *Linguistic Inquiry* 34:269–280.

Boeckx, Cedric, and Hornstein, Norbert. 2004. Movement under Control. *Linguistic Inquiry* 35:431–452.

Boeckx, Cedric, and Hornstein, Norbert. 2006a. Control in Icelandic and Theories of Control. *Linguistic Inquiry* 37:591–606.

Boeckx, Cedric, and Hornstein, Norbert. 2006b. The Virtues of Control as Movement. *Syntax* 9:118–130.

Boeckx, Cedric, and Hornstein, Norbert. 2007. On (Non-)Obligatory Control. In *New Horizons in the Analysis of Control and Raising*, ed. William D. Davies and Stanley Dubinsky, 251–262. Dordrecht: Springer.

Boeckx, Cedric, Hornstein, Norbert, and Nunes, Jairo. 2010a. Icelandic Control Really Is A-movement: Reply to Bobaljik and Landau. *Linguistic Inquiry* 41:111–130.

Boeckx, Cedric, Hornstein, Norbert, and Nunes, Jairo. 2010b. *Control as Movement*. Cambridge: Cambridge University Press.

Bondaruk, Anna. 2004. *PRO and Control in English, Irish and Polish: A Minimalist Analysis*. Lublin: Wydawinctwo KUL.

Bondaruk, Anna. 2006. The Licensing of Subjects and Objects in Irish Non-finite Clauses. *Lingua* 116:874–894.

Bošković, Željko. 1996. Selection and the Categorial Status of Infinitival Complements. *Natural Language & Linguistic Theory* 14:269–304.

Bouchard, Denis. 1984. *On the Content of Empty Categories*. Dordrecht: Foris.

Bouchard, Denis. 1985. PRO, Pronominal or Anaphor. *Linguistic Inquiry* 16:471–477.

Bowers, John. 1973. *Grammatical Relations*. PhD dissertation, MIT.

Bowers, John. 1981. *The Theory of Grammatical Relations*. Ithaca, IY: Cornell University Press.

Brame, Michael K. 1976. *Conjectures and Refutations in Syntax and Semantics*. Amsterdam: North-Holland.

Bresnan, Joan. 1978. A Realistic Transformational Grammar. In *Linguistic Theory and Psychological Reality*, ed. Morris Halle, Joan Bresnan, and George A. Miller, 1–60. Cambridge, MA: MIT Press.

Bresnan, Joan. 1982. Control and Complementation. *Linguistic Inquiry* 13:343–434.

Burukina, Irina. 2023. External Merge in Spec, CP: Complementizers Projecting an Argument. *Syntax* 26:85–105.

Charnavel, Isabelle. 2019. *Locality and Logophoricity: A Theory of Exempt Anaphora*. Oxford: Oxford University Press.

Chierchia, Gennaro. 1984. *Topics in the Syntax and Semantics of Infinitives and Gerunds*. PhD dissertation, UMASS, Amherst, MA.

Chierchia, Gennaro. 1990. Anaphora and Attitudes *De Se*. In *Semantics and Contextual Expression*, ed. Renate Bartsch, Johan van Benthem, and Peter van Emde Boas, 1–32. Dordrecht: Foris.

Chomsky, Noam. 1955. *The Logical Structure of Linguistic Theory*. Ms. MIT. (Published by) New York: Plenum Press, 1975.

Chomsky, Noam. 1965. *Aspects of the Theory of Syntax*. Cambridge, MA: MIT Press.

Chomsky, Noam. 1973. Conditions on Transformations. In *A Festschrift for Morris Halle*, ed. Stephen R. Anderson and Paul Kiparsky. New York: Holt, Rinehart and Winston. Reprinted in Noam Chomsky, ed. (1977), *Essays on Form and Interpretation*, pp. 81–160. New York: North-Holland.

Chomsky, Noam. 1980. On Binding. *Linguistic Inquiry* 11:1–46.

Chomsky, Noam. 1981. *Lectures on Government and Binding*. Berlin: Mouton de Gruyter.

Chomsky, Noam. 1991. Some Notes on Economy of Derivation and Representation. In *Principles and Parameters in Comparative Grammar*, ed. Robert Freidin, 417–454. Cambridge, MA: MIT Press.

Chomsky, Noam. 1995. *The Minimalist Program*. Cambridge, MA: MIT Press.

Chomsky, Noam, and Lasnik, Howard. 1977. Filters and Control. *Linguistic Inquiry* 8:425–504.

Chomsky, Noam. 2021. Minimalism: Where Are We Now, and Where Can We Hope to Go. *Genko Kenkyu* 160:1–41.

Chomsky, Noam, Seely, T. Daniel, Berwick, Robert C., Fong, Sandiway, Huybregts, M. A. C., Kitahara, Hisatsugu, McInnerney, Andrew, and

Sugimoto, Yushi. 2023. *Merge and the Strong Minimalist Thesis*: Elements in Generative Syntax. Cambridge: Cambridge University Press.

Chomsky, Noam. 2024. The Miracle Creed and SMT. In *A Cartesian Dream: A Geometrical Account of Syntax: In honor of Andrea Moro*, eds. Matteo Greco and Davide Mocci, 17–40: LingBuzz Press.

Citko, Barbara. 2012. Control and Obviation: A View from Polish. Paper presented in *SinFonIJA 5*, University of Vienna.

Clark, Robin. 1990. *Thematic Theory in Syntax and Interpretation*. London: Routledge.

Collins, Chris, and Postal, Paul M. 2012. *Imposters: A Study of Pronominal Agreement*. Cambridge, MA: MIT Press.

Comrie, Bernard. 1981. *Language Universals and Linguistic Typology: Syntax and Morphology*. Oxford: Basil Blackwell.

Culicover, Peter W., and Jackendoff, Ray. 2001. Control Is Not Movement. *Linguistic Inquiry* 32:493–512.

Culicover, Peter W., and Jackendoff, Ray. 2006. Turn Over Control to Semantics. *Syntax* 9:131–152.

Culicover, Peter W., and Wilkins, Wendy. 1986. Control, PRO and the Projection Principle. *Language* 62:120–153.

Cysouw, Michael. 2003. *The Paradigmatic Structure of Person Marking*. Oxford: Oxford University Press.

Dalrymple, Mary. 2001. *Lexical Functional Grammar: Syntax and Semantics*, Vol. 34. San Diego, CA: Academic Press.

Davies, William D., and Dubinsky, Stanley. 2004. *The Grammar of Raising and Control: A Course in Syntactic Argumentation*. Oxford: Blackwell.

Deal, Amy Rose. 2020. *A Theory of Indexical Shift: Meaning, Grammar and Crosslinguistics Variation*. Cambridge, MA: MIT Press.

Donaldson, James. 2021. *Control in Free Adjuncts: The "Dangling Modifier" in English*. PhD dissertation, University of Edinburgh.

Douglas, Jamie. 2018. Control into Infinitival Relatives. *English Language and Linguistics* 23:469–494.

Dowty, David. 1985. On Recent Analyses of the Semantics of Control. *Linguistics and Philosophy* 8:291–331.

DuBois, John W. 1987. The Discourse Basis of Ergativity. *Language* 63:805–855.

Duffley, Patrick J. 2014. *Reclaiming Control as a Semantic and Pragmatic Phenomenon*. Amsterdam: John Benjamins.

Erteschik-Shir, Nomi. 1997. *The Dynamics of Focus Structure*. Cambridge: Cambridge University Press.

Español-Echevarría, Manuel. 2000. The Interaction of Obligatory and Nonobligatory Control in Rationale Clauses. In *Proceedings of WCCFL 19*, ed. Roger Billerey and Brook Danielle Lillehaugen, 97–110. Somerville, MA: Cascadilla Press.

Farkas, Donca F. 1988. On Obligatory Control. *Linguistics and Philosophy* 11:27–58.

Ferreira, Marcelo. 2009. Null Subjects and Finite Control in Brazilian Portuguese. In *Minimalist Essays on Brazilian Portuguese Syntax*, ed. Jairo Nunes, 17–49. Amsterdam: John Benjamins.

Fischer, Silke. 2018. Locality, Control, and Non-adjoined Islands. *Glossa* 3(1):82. doi: https://doi.org/10.5334/gjgl.182.

Fischer, Silke, and Flaate Høyem, Inghild. 2022. Adjunct Control in German, Norwegian, and English. *Journal of Linguistics* 25:1–41.

Fukuda, Shinichiro. 2008. Backward Control. *Language and Linguistics Compass* 2:168–195.

Ganenkov, Dmitry. 2023. Partial Control with Overt Embedded Subjects in Chirag. *Language* 99:457–490.

Givón, Talmy. 1976. Topic, Pronoun and Grammatical Agreement. In *Subject and Topic*, ed. Charles N. Li, 151–188. New York: Academic Press.

Grano, Thomas. 2017a. What Partial Control Might Not Tell Us about Agreement: A Reply to Landau. *Syntax* 20:400–413.

Grano, Thomas. 2017b. Control, Temporal Orientation, and the Cross-Linguistic Grammar of Trying. *Glossa* 2(1): 94. doi: https://doi.org/10.5334/gjgl.335.

Grano, Thomas A. 2015. *Control and Restructuring*. Oxford: Oxford University Press.

Green, Jeffrey J. 2018. *Adjunct Control: Syntax and Processing*. PhD dissertation, University of Maryland.

Green, Jeffrey J. 2019. A Movement Theory of Adjunct Control. *Glossa* 4(1): 87:1–34.

Grimshaw, Jane. 1994. Minimal Projection and Clause Structure. In *Syntactic Theory and First Language Acquisition: Cross Linguistic Perspectives – Volume I: Heads, Projections and Learnability*, ed. Barbara Lust, Margarita Suñer, and Jonh Whitman, 75–83. Hillsdale, NJ: Erlbaum.

Haegeman, Liliane, and Hill, Virginia. 2013. The Syntactization of Discourse. In *Syntax and Its Limits*, ed. Raffaella Folli, Christina Sevdali, and Robert Truswell, 370–390. Oxford: Oxford University Press.

Halpert, Claire. 2019. Raising, Unphased. *Natural Language & Linguistic Theory* 37:123–165.

Han, Chung-hye, and Storoshenko, Dennis Ryan. 2012. Semantic Binding of Long-Distance Anaphor *caki* in Korean. *Language* 88:764–790.

Hasegawa, Nobuko. 2009. Agreement at the CP Level: Clause Types and the "Person" Restriction on the Subject. In *Proceedings of the Workshop on*

Altaic Formal Linguistic 5, ed. Ryosuke Shibagaki and Reiko Vermeulen, 131–152. Cambridge, MA: MITWPL.

Heim, Irene. 1994. Puzzling Reflexive Pronouns in *De Se* Reports. Unpublished handout presented at Bielefield. Cambridge, MA: MIT Press.

Heim, Irene. 2008. Features on Bound Pronouns. In *Phi Theory: Phi-Features across Modules and Interfaces*, ed. Daniel Harbour, David Adger, and Susana Béjar, 35–56. Oxford, NY: Oxford University Press.

Herbeck, Peter. 2021. The (Null) Subject of Adjunct Infinitives in Spoken Spanish. In *Non-canonical Control in a Cross-Linguistic Perspective*, ed. Anne Mucha, Jutta M. Hartmann, and Beata Trawiński, 259–286. Amsterdam: John Benjamins.

Hill, Virginia. 2007. Vocatives and the Pragmatics – Syntax Interface. *Lingua* 117:2077–2105.

Hintzen, Wolfram, and Martin, Txuss. 2021. *De Se* or Not *De Se*: A Question of Grammar. *Language Sciences* 85:101343.

Hornstein, Norbert. 1999. Movement and Control. *Linguistic Inquiry* 30:69–96.

Hornstein, Norbert. 2003. On Control. In *Minimalist Syntax*, ed. Randall Hendrick, 6–81. Oxford: Blackwell.

Hornstein, Norbert, and Polinsky, Maria. 2010. Control as Movement: Across Languages and Constructions. In *Movement Theory of Control*, ed. Norbert Hornstein and Maria Polinsky, 1–41. Amsterdam: John Benjamins.

Huang, C.-T. James. 1989. Pro-drop in Chinese: A Generalized Control Theory. In *The Null Subject Parameter*, ed. Osvaldo Jaeggli and Kenneth J. Safir, 185–214. Dordrecht: Kluwer Academic.

Huang, Yan. 1994. *The Syntax and Pragmatics of Anaphora*. Cambridge: Cambridge University Press.

Jackendoff, Ray. 1974. A Deep Structure Projection Rule. *Linguistic Inquiry* 5:481–506.

Jackendoff, Ray, and Culicover, Peter W. 2003. The Semantic Basis of Control in English. *Language* 79:517–556.

Jacobson, Pauline. 1992. Raising without Movement. In *Control and Grammar*, ed. Richard Larson, Sabine Iatridou, Utpal Lahiri, and James Higginbotham, 149–194. Dordrecht: Kluwer Academic.

Janke, Vikki, and Bailey, Laura R. 2017. Effects of Discourse on Control. *Journal of Linguistics* 53:533–565.

Jenks, Peter, and Rose, Sharon. 2017. Documenting Raising and Control in Moro. In *Africa's Endangered Languages: Documentary and Theoretical Approaches*, ed. Jason Kandybowicz and Harold Torrence, 207–236. Oxford: Oxford University Press.

Jones, Charles. 1992. Comments on Goodluck and Behne. In *Theoretical Issues in Language Acquisition*, eds. Jürgen Weissenborn, Helen Goodluck and Thomas Roeper, 173–189. Hillsdale, NJ: Erlbaum.

Kawasaki, Noriko. 1993. *Control and Arbitrary Interpretation in English*. PhD dissertation, UMASS.

Kirby, Susannah, Davies, William D., and Dubinsky, Stanley. 2010. Up to D[eb]ate on Raising and Control. *Language and Linguistics Compass* 4:390–416.

Kiss, Tibor. 2004. On the Empirical Viability of the Movement Theory of Control. Ms., *Ms*. Ruhr-Universität Bochum.

Kortmann, Bernd. 1991. *Free Adjuncts and Absolutes in English: Problems of Control and Interpretation*. New York: Routledge.

Koster, Jan. 1984. On Binding and Control. *Linguistic Inquiry* 15:417–459.

Kratzer, Angelika. 2009. Making a Pronoun: Fake Indexicals as Windows into the Properties of Pronouns. *Linguistic Inquiry* 40:187–237.

Kuno, Susumu. 1972. Pronominalization, Reflexivization, and Direct Discourse. *Linguistic Inquiry* 3:161–195.

Kuno, Susumu. 1975. Super Equi-NP Deletion Is a Pseudo-Transformation. In *Proceedings of North Eastern Linguistic Society 5*, 29–44. UMASS, Amherst, MA: GLSA.

Kuno, Susumu. 2006. Empathy and Direct Discourse Perspectives. In *Handbook of Pragmatics*, ed. Larry R. Horn and Gregory Ward, 315–343. Oxford: Blackwell.

Kwon, Nayoung, Monahan, Philip J., and Polinsky, Maria. 2010. Object Control in Korean: A Backward Control Impostor. In *Movement Theory of Control*, ed. Norbert Hornstein and Maria Polinsky, 299–328. Amsterdam: John Benjamins.

Landau, Idan. 2000. *Elements of Control: Structure and Meaning in Infinitival Constructions*. Dordrecht: Kluwer Academic.

Landau, Idan. 2001. Control and Extraposition: The Case of Super-Equi. *Natural Language and Linguistic Theory* 19:109–152.

Landau, Idan. 2002. (Un)interpretable Neg in Comp. *Linguistic Inquiry* 33:465–492.

Landau, Idan. 2003. Movement Out of Control. *Linguistic Inquiry* 34:471–498.

Landau, Idan. 2004. The Scale of Finiteness and the Calculus of Control. *Natural Language and Linguistic Theory* 22:811–877.

Landau, Idan. 2006. Severing the Distribution of PRO from Case. *Syntax* 9:153–170.

Landau, Idan. 2007. Movement-Resistant Aspects of Control. In *New Horizons in the Analysis of Control and Raising*, eds. William D. Davies and Stanley Dubinsky, 293–325. Dordrecht: Springer.

Landau, Idan. 2008. Two Routes of Control: Evidence from Case Transmission in Russian. *Natural Language and Linguistic Theory* 26:877–924.

Landau, Idan. 2010. The Explicit Syntax of Implicit Arguments. *Linguistic Inquiry* 41:357–388.

Landau, Idan. 2013. *Control in Generative Grammar: A Research Companion.* Cambridge: Cambridge University Press.

Landau, Idan. 2015. *A Two-Tiered Theory of Control.* Cambridge, MA: MIT Press.

Landau, Idan. 2016a. Against the Null Comitative Analysis of Partial Control. *Linguisic Inquiry* 47:572–580.

Landau, Idan. 2016b. Agreement at PF: An Argument from Partial Control. *Syntax* 19:79–109.

Landau, Idan. 2017. Adjunct Control Depends on Voice. In *A Pesky Set: Papers for David Pesetsky*, ed. Claire Halpert, Hadas Kotek, and Coppe van Urk, 93–102. Cambridge, MA: MITWPL.

Landau, Idan. 2018. Direct Variable Binding and Agreement in Obligatory Control. In *Pronouns in Embedded Contexts*, ed. Pritty Patel-Grosz, Patrick Georg Grosz, and Sarah Zobel, 1–41. Dordrecht: Springer.

Landau, Idan. 2020. Nonobligatory Control with Communication Verbs: New Evidence and Implications. *Linguistic Inquiry* 51:75–96.

Landau, Idan. 2021a. *A Selectional Theory of Adjunct Control.* Cambridge, MA: MIT Press.

Landau, Idan. 2021b. Duality of Control in Gerundive Complements of P. *Journal of Linguistics* 57:783–813.

Landau, Idan. 2024. Noncanonical Obligatory Control. *Language and Linguistics Compass* e12515. https://doi.org/10.1111/lnc3.12515.

Landau, Idan. Empirical Challenges to the Form-Copy Theory of Control. To appear in *Glossa.*

Larson, Richard. 1991. Promise and the Theory of Control. *Linguistic Inquiry* 22:103–139.

Lebeaux, David. 1984. Anaphoric Binding and the Definition of PRO. In *Proceedings of North Eastern Linguistic Society 14*, ed. Charles Jones and Peter Sells, 253–274. UMASS, Amherst, MA: GLSA.

Lee, Kum Young. 2009. *Finite Control in Korean.* PhD dissertation, University of Iowa.

Legate, Julie. 2021. Noncanonical Passives: A Typology of Voices in an Impoverished Universal Grammar. *Annual Reviews* 7:157–176.

Leung, Tommi, and Halefom, Girma. 2017. The Theory and Syntactic Representation of Control Structures: An Analysis from Amharic. *Glossa* 2(1):97:1–33.

Liao, Wei-wen, and Wang, Yuyun. 2022. Attitude, Control, and the Finiteness Distinction in Chinese. Research Square. https://doi.org/10.21203/rs.3.rs-1706057/v1

Lohninger, Madgalena, and Wurmbrand, Susi. 2024. Typology of Argument Clauses. In *Handbook of Clausal Embedding*, ed. Anton Benz, Werner Frey, Manfred Krifka, Thomas McFadden, Marzena Żygis. Berlin: Language Science Press.

Lyngfelt, Benjamin. 2000. OT Semantics and Control. Ms., *Ms.* Göteborg University.

Lyngfelt, Benjamin. 2009. Towards a Comprehensive Construction Grammar Account of Control: A Case Study of Swedish Infinitives. *Constructions and Frames* 1:153–189.

Madigan, Sean. 2008a. *Control Constructions in Korean*. PhD dissertation, University of Delaware.

Madigan, Sean. 2008b. Obligatory Split Control into Exhortative Complements in Korean. *Linguistic Inquiry* 39:493–502.

Manzini, M. Rita. 1983. On Control and Control Theory. *Linguistic Inquiry* 14:421–446.

Manzini, M. Rita, and Roussou, Anna. 2000. A Minimalist Theory of A-movement and Control. *Lingua* 110:409–447.

Manzini, M. Rita, and Savoia, L. Maria. 2018. Finite and Non-finite Complementation, Particles and Control in Aromanian, Compared to Other Romance Varieties and Albanian. *Linguistic Variation* 18:215–264.

Martin, Roger A. 1996. *A Minimalist Theory of PRO and Control*. PhD dissertation, UCONN.

Martins, Ana Maria, and Nunes, Jairo. 2017. Identity Avoidance with Reflexive Clitics in European Portuguese and Minimalist Approaches to Control. *Linguistic Inquiry* 48:627–649.

Matsuda, Asako. 2019. *Person in Partial Control*. PhD dissertation, Ochanomizu University.

Matsuda, Asako. 2021. Control from Inside: Evidence from Japanese. In *Non-canonical Control in a Cross-Linguistic Perspective*, ed. Anne Mucha, Jutta M. Hartmann, and Beata Trawiński, 137–165. Amsterdam: John Benjamins.

McCloskey, James. 1980a. Is There Raising in Modern Irish? *Ériu* 31:59–99.

McCloskey, James. 1980b. A Note on Modern Irish Verbal Nouns and the VP-Complement Analysis. *Linguistic Analysis* 6:345–357.

McCloskey, James. 1985. Case, Movement and Raising in Moder Irish. In *Proceedings of WCCFL 4*, ed. Jeffrey Goldberg, Susannah Mackaye, and Wescoat Michael, 190–205. Stanford, CA: Stanford Linguistics Association.

McCloskey, James, and Sells, Peter. 1988. Control and A-chains in Modern Irish. *Natural Language and Linguistic Theory* 6:143–189.

McFadden, Thomas. 2014. On Subject Reference and the Cartography of Clause Types. *Natural Language & Linguistic Theory* 32:115–135.

McFadden, Thomas, and Sundaresan, Sandhya. 2018. Reducing *pro* and PRO to a Single Source. *The Linguistic Review* 35:463–518.

Meinunger, André. 2006. Interface Restrictions on Verb Second. *Linguistic Review* 23:127–160.

Modesto, Marcello. 2010. What Brazilian Portuguese Says about Control: Remarks on Boeckx & Hornstein. *Syntax* 13:78–96.

Modesto, Marcello. 2018. Inflected Infinitives in Brazilian Portuguese and the Theory of Control. In *Complement Clauses in Portuguese: Syntax and Acquisition*, ed. Ana Lúcia Santos and Anabela Gonçalves, 59–100. Amsterdam: John Benjamins.

Mohanan, K. P. 1982. Infinitival Subjects, Government and Abstract Case. *Linguistic Inquiry* 13:323–327.

Mohanan, K. P. 1983. Functional and Anaphoric Control. *Linguistic Inquiry* 14:641–674.

Moltmann, Friederike. 2006. Generic One, Arbitrary PRO, and the First Person. *Natural Language Semantics* 14:257–281.

Morgan, Jerry L. 1970. On the Criterion of Identity for Noun Phrase Deletion. In *Proceedings of CLS 6*, ed. Mary Ann Campbell, Lindholm James, Davison Alice et al., 380–389. Chicago, IL: Chicago University Press.

Mucha, Anne, and Hartmann, Jutta M. 2022. (Non)Attitude Verbs and Control Shift: Evidence from German. In *Proceedings of Sinn und Bedeutung 26*, ed. Daniel Gutzmann and Sophie Repp, 622–640. Konstanz: University of Konstanz.

Ndayiragije, Juvénal. 2012. On Raising Out of Control. *Linguistic Inquiry* 43:275–299.

Nishigauchi, Taisuke. 1984. Control and the Thematic Domain. *Language* 60:215–250.

Nishigauchi, Taisuke. 2014. Reflexive Binding: Awareness and Empathy from a Syntactic Point of View. *Journal of East Asian Linguistics* 23:157–206.

Noyer, Rolf. 1992. *Features, Positions and Affixes in Autonomous Morphological Structure*. PhD dissertation, MIT.

Pak, Miok, Portner, Paul, and Zanuttini, Raffaella. 2008. Agreement in Promissive, Imperative, and Exhortative Clauses. *Korean Linguistics* 14:157–175.

Pearson, Hazel. 2013. *The Sense of Self: Topics in the Semantics of De Se Expressions*. PhD dissertation, Harvard University.

Pearson, Hazel. 2016. The Semantics of Partial Control. *Natural Language and Linguistic Theory* 34:691–738.

Pearson, Hazel. 2018. Counterfactual *de se*. *Semantics and Pragmatics* 11. https://doi.org/10.3765/sp.3711.3762.

Pearson, Hazel, and Roeper, Tom. 2022. Excluded Entailments and the De Se/ De Re Partition. *Inquiry* 65:858–886.

Percus, Orin, and Sauerland, Uli. 2003. On the LFs of Attitude Reports. In *Proceedings of Sinn and Bedeutung 7*, ed. Matthias Weisberger, 228–242. Konstanz: Universität Konstanz.

Pitteroff, Marcel, Alexiadou, Artemis, Darby, Jeannique, and Fischer, Silke. 2017. On Partial Control in German. *Journal of Comparative Germanic Linguistics* 20:139–185.

Pitteroff, Marcel, and Sheehan, Michelle. 2018. The Case for Fake Partial Control in French and German In *Proceedings of NELS 48*, eds. Sherry Hucklebridge and Max Nelson, 245–258. Amherst, MA: GLSA Publications.

Pietraszko, Asia. 2021. Backward Control without A-movement or φ-agreement. In *Proceedings of NELS 51*, eds. Alessa Farinella and Angelica Hill, 139–152. Amherst, MA: GLSA Publications.

Pires, Acrisio. 2007. The Derivation of Clausal Gerunds. *Syntax* 10:165–203.

Pitteroff, Marcel, and Schäfer, Florian. 2019. Implicit Control Cross-Linguistically. *Language* 95:136–184.

Polinsky, Maria. 2013. Raising and Control. In *The Cambridge Handbook of Generative Syntax*, ed. Marcel den Dikken, 577–606. Cambridge: Cambridge University Press.

Polinsky, Maria, and Potsdam, Eric. 2002. Backward Control. *Linguistic Inquiry* 33:245–282.

Postal, Paul. 1970. On Coreferential Complement Subject Deletion. *Linguistic Inquiry* 1:439–500.

Postal, Paul M. 1974. *On Raising*. Cambridge, MA: MIT Press.

Postal, Paul M., and Pullum, Geoffrey K. 1988. Expletive Noun Phrases in Subcategorized Positions. *Linguistic Inquiry* 19:635–670.

Potsdam, Eric. 2009. Malagasy Backward Object Control. *Language* 85:754–784.

Potsdam, Eric, and Haddad, Youssef A. 2017. Control Phenomena. In *The Wiley Blackwell Companion to Syntax*, ed. Martin Everaert and Henk van Riemsdijk. New York: John Wiley & Sons.

Quirk, Randolph, Greenbaum, Sidney, Leach, Jeoffrey, and Svartvik, Jan. 1985. *A Comprehensive Grammar of the English Language*. London: Longman.

Reed, Lisa A. 2018. Against Control by Implicit Passive Agents. In *Romance Languages and Linguistic Theory 14: Selected Papers from the 46th*

Linguistic Symposium on Romance Languages (LSRL), ed. Lori Repetti and Francisco Ordóñez, 279–292. Amsterdam: John Benjamins.

Rizzi, Luigi. 1986. On Chain Formation. In *Syntax and Semantics 19: The Syntax of Pronominal Clitics*, ed. Hagit Borer, 65–95. New York: Academic Press.

Rizzi, Luigi. 1997. The Fine Structure of the Left Periphery. In *Elements of Grammar: Handbook in Generative Syntax*, ed. Liliane Haegeman, 281–337. Dordrecht: Kluwer Academic.

Rodrigues, Cilene. 2004. *Impoverished Morphology and A-movement out of Case Domains*. PhD dissertation, University of Maryland.

Rodrigues, Cilene. 2007. Agreement and Flotation in Partial and Inverse Partial Control Configurations. In *New Horizons in the Analysis of Control and Raising*, ed. William D. Davies and Stanley Dubinsky, 213–229. Dordrecht: Springer.

Rooryck, Johan. 2000. *Configurations of Sentential Complementation: Perspectives from Romance Languages*. London: Routledge.

Rooryck, Johan. 2007. Control via Selection. In *New Horizons in the Analysis of Control and Raising*, ed. William D. Davies and Stanley Dubinsky, 281–292. Dordrecht: Springer.

Rosenbaum, Peter. 1967. *The Grammar of English Predicate Complement Constructions*. Cambridge, MA: MIT Press.

Rosenbaum, Peter. 1970. A Principle Governing Deletion in English Sentential Complementation. In *Readings in English Transformational Grammar*, ed. Roderick Jacobs and Peter Rosenbaum, 220–229. Waltham, MA: Ginn-Blaisdell.

Runner, Jeffrey T. 2006. Lingering Challenges to the Raising-to-Object and Object-Control Constructions. *Syntax* 9:193–213.

Růžička, Rudolph. 1999. *Control in Grammar and Pragmatics: A Cross-Linguistic Study*. Amsterdam: John Benjamins.

Safir, Ken. 1985. *Syntactic Chains*. Cambridge: Cambridge University Press.

Safir, Ken. 1993. Perception, Selection, and Structural Economy. *Natural Language Semantics* 2:47–70.

Safir, Ken. 2004. Person, Context and Perspective. *Rivista di Linguistica* 16:107–153.

Sag, Ivan, and Pollard, Carl. 1991. An Integrated Theory of Complement Control. *Language* 67:63–113.

Satik, Deniz. 2019. Control Is Not Movement: Evidence from Overt PRO in Ewe. Ms., Harvard University.

Sato, Yosuke. 2011. On the Movement Theory of Control: Voices from Standard Indonesian. *Canadian Journal of Linguistics* 56:267–275.

Schlenker, Philippe. 2003. A Plea for Monsters. *Linguistics and Philosophy* 26:29–120.

Schlenker, Philippe. 2011. Indexicality and *De Se* Reports. In *Semantics: An International Handbook of Natural Language Meaning*, ed. Klaus von Heusinger, Claudia Maienborn, and Paul Portner, 1561–1604. Berlin: Mouton de Gruyter.

Seo, Saetbyol, and Hoe, Semoon. 2015. Agreement of Point-of-Viewer and a Jussive Subject. *Studies in Generative Grammar* 25:1–34.

Sharvit, Yael. 2011. Covaluation and Unexpected BT Effects. *Journal of Semantics* 28:55–106.

Sheehan, Michelle. 2012. A New Take on Partial Control: Defective Thematic Intervention. *Cambridge Occasional Papers in Linguistics* 6:1–47.

Sheehan, Michelle. 2014. Partial Control in the Romance Languages: The Covert Comitative Analysis. In *Romance Languages and Linguistic Theory 2012: Papers from 'Going Romance' Leuven 2012*, eds. Karen Lahousse and Stefania Marzo, 181–198. Amsterdam: John Benjamins.

Sheehan, Michelle. 2018a. Control of Inflected Infinitives in European Portuguese. In *Complement Clauses in Portuguese: Syntax and Acquisition*, eds. Anabela Gonçalves and Ana Lúcia Santos, 29–58. Amsterdam: John Benjamins.

Sheehan, Michelle. 2018b. On the Difference Between Exhaustive and Partial Control. In *Null Suibjects in generative Grammar: A Synchronic and Diachronic Perspective*, eds. Federica Cognola and Jan Casalicchio, 141–170. Oxford: Oxford University Press.

Sigurðsson, Einar F., and Wood, Jim. 2021. On the Implicit Argument of Icelandic Indirect Causatives. *Linguistic Inquiry* 52:579–625.

Sigurðsson, Halldór A. 2008. The Case of PRO. *Natural Language and Linguistic Theory* 26:403–450.

Sigurðsson, Halldór A. 2011. Conditions on Argument Drop. *Linguisic Inquiry* 42:267–304.

Sisovics, Milena. 2018. *Embedded Jussives as Instances of Control: The Case of Mongolian and Korean*. PhD dissertation, MIT.

Song, Jae Jung. 2001. *Linguistic Typology: Morphology and Syntax*. London: Pearson Education.

Speas, Margaret. 2004. Evidentiality, Logophoricity and Syntactic Representation of Ptagmatic Features. *Lingua* 114:255–276.

Speas, Margaret. 2006. Economy, Agreement, and the Representation of Null Arguments. In *Arguments and Agreement*, ed. Peter Ackema, Patrick Brandt, Maaike Schoorlemmer, and Fred Weerman, 35–75. Oxford: Oxford University Press.

Stegovec, Adrian. 2019. Perspectival Control and Obviation in Directive Clauses. *Natural Language Semantics* 27:47–94.

Stephenson, Tamina. 2010. Control in Centred Worlds. *Journal of Semantics* 27:409–436.

Stiebels, Barbara. 2007. Towards a Typology of Complement Control. *ZAS Working Papers in Linguistics* 47: 1–59. https://doi.org/10.21248/zaspil.47.2007.344.

Stiebels, Barbara. 2015. Control. In *Syntax – Theory and Analysis*, ed. Tibor Kiss and Artemis Alexiadou, 412–446. Berlin: de Gruyter.

Sundaresan, Sandhya. 2014. Making Sense of Silence: Finiteness and the (OC) PRO vs. *pro* Distinction. *Natural Language & Linguistic Theory* 32:59–85.

Sundaresan, Sandhya. 2018. Perspective Is Syntactic: Evidence from Anaphora. *Glossa* 3(1):128:1–40.

Sundaresan, Sandhya. 2021. Shifty Attitudes: Indexical Shift versus Perspectival Anaphora. *Annual Review of Linguistics* 7:235–259.

Sundaresan, Sandhya, and McFadden, Thomas. 2009. Subject Distribution in Tamil and Other Languages: Selection vs. Case. *Journal of South Asian Linguistics* 2:5–34.

Swierskia, Anna. 2004. *Person*. Cambridge: Cambridge University Press.

Szabolcsi, Anna. 2009. Overt Nominative Subjects in Infinitival Complements: Data, Diagnostics, and Preliminary Analyses. In *NYU Working Papers in Linguistics, Vol. 2: Papers in Syntax*, ed. Patricia Irwin and Violeta Vasquéz Rojas Maldonado. New York: New York University.

Thráinsson, Höskuldur. 1979. *On Complementation in Icelandic*. New York: Garland Press.

Truswell, Robert. 2013. Reconstruction, Control and Movement. In *Syntax and Its Limits*, ed. Raffaella R. Folli, Christina Sevdali, Robert Truswell, 44–65. Oxford: Oxford University Press.

Uegaki, Wataru. 2011. Controller Shift in Centered-World Semantics. Ms., MIT.

Ussery, Cherlon. 2008. What It Means to Agree: The Behavior of Case and Phi Features in Icelandic Control. In *Proceedings of WCCFL 26*, ed. Charles B. Chang and Hannah J. Haynie, 480–488. Somerville, MA: Cascadilla Press.

van Urk, Coppe. 2013. Visser's Generalization: The Syntax of Control and the Passive. *Linguistic Inquiry* 44:168–178.

Vanden Wyngaerd, Guido J. 1994. *PRO-legomena*. Berlin: Mouton de Gruyter.

von Stechow, Arnim. 2003. Feature Deletion under Semantic Binding. In *Proceedings of NELS 33*, ed. Makoto Kadowaki and Shigeto Kawahara, 377–403. Amherst, MA: GLSA.

Vinka, Mikael. 2022. Two Types of Null Subjects in South Saami. In *Null Subjects in Slavic and Finno-Ugric: Licensing, Structure and Typology*, eds. Gréte Dalmi, Egor Tsedryk and Piotr Cegłowski, 307–346. Berlin, Boston: De Gruyter Mouton.

Wechsler, Stephen. 2010. What 'You' and 'I' Mean to Each Other: Person Indexicals, Self-Ascription and Theory of Mind. *Language* 86:332–365.

Wexler, Ken, and Culicover, Peter. 1980. *Formal Principles of Language Acquisition*. Cambridge, MA: MIT Press.

White, Aaron S., and Grano, Thomas A. 2014. An Experimental Investigation of Partial Control. In *Proceedings of Sinn und Bedeutung 18*, ed. Anamaria Fălăuş Urtzi Etxeberria, Aritz Irurtzun, and Bryan Leferman, 469–486. Konstanz: University of Konstanz.

Wilkinson, Robert. 1971. Complement Subject Deletion and Subset Relations. *Linguistic Inquiry* 2:575–584.

Williams, Edwin. 1980. Predication. *Linguistic Inquiry* 11:203–238.

Williams, Edwin. 1992. Adjunct Control. In *Control and Grammar*, ed. Richard Larson, Sabine Iatridou, Utpal Lahiri, and James Higginbotham, 297–322. Dordrecht: Kluwer Academic.

Wiltschko, Martina, and Heim, Johannes. 2016. The Syntax of Confirmationals: A Neo-performative Analysis. In *Outside the Clause: Form and Function of Extra-Clausal Constituents*, ed. Gunther Kaltenböck, Evelien Keizer, and Arne Lohmann, 305–340. Amsterdam: John Benjamins.

Wood, Jim. 2012. Against the Movement Theory of Control: Another Argument from Icelandic. *Linguistic Inquiry* 43:322–330.

Woods, Rebecca. 2021. Towards a Model of the Syntax – Discourse Interface: A Syntactic Analysis of *Please*. *English Language & Linguistics* 25:121–153.

Wurmbrand, Susi. 1999. Modal Verbs Must Be Raising Verbs. In *Proceedings of WCCFL 18*, ed. Sonya Bird, Andrew Carnie, Jason D. Haugen, and Peter Norquest, 599–612. Somerville, MA: Cascadilla Press.

Wurmbrand, Susi. 2002. Semantic vs. Syntactic Control. In *Proceedings of the 15th Workshop on Comparative Germanic Syntax*, ed. Jan-Wouter Zwart and Werner Abraham, 93–127. Amsterdam: John Benjamins.

Wurmbrand, Susi. 2003. *Infinitives: Restructuring and Clause Structure*. New York: Mouton de Gruyter.

Wurmbrand, Susi. 2015. Restructuring Cross-Linguistically. In *Proceedings of the NELS 45*, ed. Thuy Bui and Deniz Özyıldız, 227–240. Amherst, MA: GLSA.

Wurmbrand, Susi. 2019. Cross-Clausal A-dependencies. In *Proceedings of CLS 54*, ed. Eszter Ronai, Laura Stigliano, and Yenan Sun, 585–604. Chicago, IL: Chicago Linguistic Society.

Xu, Leijiong. 1986. Towards a Lexical-Thematic Theory of Control. *Linguistic Review* 5:345–376.

Yoshimoto, Keisuke. 2013. The Syntax of Japanese *Tokoro*-Clauses: Against Control Analyses. *Lingua* 127:39–71.

Zanuttini, Rafaella. 2008. Encoding the Addressee in the Syntax: Evidence from English Imperative Subjects. *Natural Language & Linguistic Theory* 26:185–218.

Zanuttini, Rafaella, Pak, Miok, and Portner, Paul. 2012. A Syntactic Analysis of Interpretive Restrictions on Imperative, Promissive, and Exhortative Subjects. *Natural Language and Linguistic Theory* 30:1231–1274.

Zu, Vera. 2018. *Discourse Participants and the Structural Representation of Context*. PhD dissertation, New York University.

Cambridge Elements ⹀

Generative Syntax

Robert Freidin

Princeton University

Robert Freidin is Emeritus Professor of Linguistics at Princeton University. His research on syntactic theory has focused on cyclicity, case and binding, with special emphasis on the evolution of the theory from its mid-twentieth century origins and the conceptual shifts that have occurred. He is the author of *Adventures in English Syntax* (Cambridge 2020), *Syntax: Basic Concepts and Applications* (Cambridge 2012), and *Generative Grammar: Theory and its History* (Routledge 2007). He is co-editor with Howard Lasnik of *Syntax: Critical Assessments* (6 volumes) (Routledge 2006).

About the Series

Cambridge Elements in Generative Syntax presents what has been learned about natural language syntax over the past sixty-five years. It focuses on the underlying principles and processes that determine the structure of human language, including where this research may be heading in the future and what outstanding questions remain to be answered.

Cambridge Elements ≡

Generative Syntax

Elements in the Series

Merge and the Strong Minimalist Thesis
Noam Chomsky, T. Daniel Seely, Robert C. Berwick, Sandiway Fong, M.A.C.
Huybregts, Hisatsugu Kitahara, Andrew McInnerney and Yushi Sugimoto

Coordinate Structures
Ning Zhang

Control
Idan Landau

A full series listing is available at: www.cambridge.org/EGSY

Printed in the United States
by Baker & Taylor Publisher Services